If I Should Wake
Before I Die

If I Should Wake Before I Die

Healing Words for Dying Persons

Lamont R. Satterly

Hospice Chaplain/Family Therapist

Illustrations & Cover Design by Michael J. Boyle

The SEARCH Foundation.
© Copyright 1997 by Lamont R. Satterly. All rights reserved.

Published in the United States by:
    The SEARCH Foundation
    1631 Fort Washington Avenue
    Maple Glen, Pennsylvania 19002

Illustrations & Cover Design: Michael J. Boyle

Book Design & Layout: Bill Gottshall

Portions from *A Course in Miracles* © Copyright 1975, 1st edition
Reprinted by permission of the Foundation for Inner Peace, Inc.
P. O. Box 598, Mill Valley, CA 94942

Library of Congress Cataloging in Publication Data:
    ISBN 0-9636686-2-5
    Satterly, Lamont R.
    If I Should Wake Before I Die

Dedication
To my Father,

Who said to me, "There is nothing to be afraid of,"
and who died proving his point.

Thank you, dad, for showing me how to do it.

We fished together years ago,
and we will again cast our lines for the big one.

.

In Memory of
Robert Charles Satterly

Table of Contents

A Personal Word

The idea for this small book came from a dying man at Christmas time. He was a seventy-one year old man, who had been struggling against lung cancer for nearly eighteen months. Married with several children and grandchildren, he had finally given in to his disease and was preparing to die.

We became good friends, he and I, as we talked in his small bedroom. Since he was always cold, the heat was fierce in his room, coating the windows with steam in reaction to the cold days outside. I remember those visits as cozy, a strange description for conversations with a dying man.

It was Christmas eve day, as I was putting on my coat to leave, when he said to me, "Will you be back to see me tomorrow?"

I didn't have to think about the answer since I was very aware of my busy family schedule for the next day. "No," I told him, "but I will see you the day after Christmas." I studied his face looking for signs of disappointment, "Your wife told me you will have a house-full tomorrow."

He nodded and puffed on his oxygen for a minute. "She's right," he laughed, "it's just that I'll miss our visit," and then as a sort of after-thought he said, "I wish you had a part of you that you could leave here with me."

As I was driving away from his house, I thought about his final words. My "inner critic" began nagging at me about the unfinished project I was always going to complete but never had. For several years I had considered writing a small devotional booklet to leave with patients — something they could read at their leisure, on their own time. And each year at holiday time, my good intention of "leaving

If I Should Wake Before I Die

a piece of myself" remained a postponed idea.

So because of a patient who dared to say what he wanted, this book became a reality. And because of the hundreds of patients who became my teachers over the past decade and a half, I have written *If I Should Wake Before I Die.*

I am deeply grateful for the patients and families with whom I have worked, for the truth they have spoken, and the impact they have had on my life. The pleasure of working with the dying can only be understood by those who have experienced it. It is indeed a privilege to meet people on their greatest journey, and to walk with them toward the other side.

To be a part of a Hospice Team, whose members laugh, cry, and work together is a gift for which I will always be grateful.

So, to the patients who showed me the way so many times, and to the Eastern Montgomery County VNA Hospice Team, I express my profound appreciation and thanks.

And to my wife, Sue, a personal word of thanks and love for her deep and sensitive support.

A final note: It is my deepest belief that those who work with the dying are always working on their own death. This certainly has been my case and continues to be so. To dispel the myth that the work is depressing is one of the aims of this book. Difficult it may be, but depressing it is not. Rather to learn how to die and to work toward the full acceptance of death, seems to be the highest path to embrace life in all its fullness. Obviously there are many ways to struggle with life, death, and meaning. For me, Hospice presents the finest.

If I Should Wake Before I Die

I love Jesus, who said to us:
"Heaven and earth will pass away.
When heaven and earth have passed away,
my word will remain."
What was your word, Jesus?
Love? Forgiveness? Affection?
All your words were one word:
Wakeup.

Antonio Machado
Translated by Robert Bly

Introduction

A woman watched her husband die.

"His life force left in a blue dot," she said.

Death is simply the name we give

to the departure of the Blue Pearl from the body.

Swami Muktananda

If I Should Wake Before I Die

Everyone who reads these words is dying.

Some will leave tomorrow while others will live for another half-century. This is the nature of the world; it is the one certainty in life.

In our Western culture, we seldom give any concrete thought to the notion of death, particularly avoiding thinking about our own. There is so much to keep us busy, from television to making money, that thoughts of death rarely find their way into our conscious minds.

It is a most unpleasant subject, and as Woody Allen said, "I'm not afraid to die, I just don't want to be there when it happens."

Working with dying people for over a decade now, I have learned a lot about death and our culture. For instance, it's interesting how many families feel the need to protect each other from the truth.

I once visited a patient who was dying of a brain tumor. Each time I would ask him a question, his wife would answer.

"How are you sleeping at night?" I said to him.

"Oh," his wife immediately jumped in, "he's doing just fine at night, aren't you dear?"

"And your appetite?" I asked.

Again before the patient could open his mouth, his wife said, "It's getting so much better, isn't it dear? Why at lunch today, he ate a bowl of soup and almost a whole sandwich; then we went for a little walk around the garden."

And that's the way the visit continued. I spoke to the patient and his wife spoke for him. As I was leaving, his wife followed me onto their sunporch. Putting her hand on my arm she said, "We haven't told him about his tumor. He just wouldn't be able

Introduction

to bear it, and I know him... he would give up hope, and that would be that."

My next visit started the same way. His wife was his protective spokesperson and he the silent patient. But then the telephone rang.

As his wife left the room to answer the phone, the patient leaned forward and motioned to me to come closer to him. I scooted across the couch and he said, "I've wanted to tell you this but I've never had a chance." He looked toward the kitchen, "I have a brain tumor but she doesn't know."

When I was driving away from their house, I shook my head at the amazing ways in which we human beings attempt to protect each other from pain. What a far better world it would be, I said to myself, if we could all just tell the truth.

Then my father was diagnosed with Cancer.

And our family did much of the same thing, played many of the same protective games, and whispered quietly in the corners of the house.

Death does strange things to all of us.

So I decided to try to write some helpful thoughts for people who are dying and for those who are taking care of them. This small book was designed to help people stare at their own death and dying with honesty and hope. It is not sugar coated nor blind to the struggles that dying people endure.

It is written in a personal manner, much the same way that you might write a letter to a friend. And I've tried to stick some humor in now and again since there can be a great deal of laughter in our circumstances, no matter how deadly they may be. Humor helps us get from here to there with a little more ease.

If I Should Wake Before I Die

When I first began working with this idea, the notion of trying to write from a Spiritual perspective troubled me. There are so many different beliefs and thoughts about God, death, and afterlife, and yet, there also are numerous places where they all cross in a common point.

Therefore, I am writing with no apologies to any faith or tradition. This book is about hope and inner peace for you who are actively dying. Writing from a position that affirms the ongoingness of life, I have chosen to use prose and poetry from numerous traditions, from Christianity to Sufism to Buddhism and countless others.

There are twenty-eight different subjects discussed in these pages; not all of them will interest you. So, skip around. Read those which intrigue you, or any which may help you in areas where you are struggling.

Most of the chapters are only three or four pages, so if you are too tired to hold a book, ask a family member to read to you. It will be helpful to you both.

In Hospice work we have a saying: people die the way they live. For the most part it's true, but it doesn't have to be. If you have spent your whole life hiding from truth or avoiding facing issues, you don't have to die that way, also. There is the possibility of healing and change in the very process of dying.

This book, then, is not for everyone since there are many people who choose, for whatever reason, to look the other way when faced with their own death. There are those who do not want to read about dying or talk about funerals, particularly their own. And that's fine. You can die however you want to die.

Introduction

But if you're looking for an anchor in the midst of the tremendous shifts in your life at this time, you will find solid places to seize in these pages. Equally, if you're looking for words of inspiration from universal scriptures, thoughts which can carry you through to the other side, they can be found at the end of every chapter.

Finally, a word about the underlying beliefs presented in these pages. I believe in the continuation of life from this somewhat feeble, material existence to the loving and peace-filled world of the Spiritual kingdom. When I was a child I used to believe that I was a body who had a soul living within. Now, I recognize that I am a soul who happens to use my body to transport me around from place to place. First and foremost, I am a spiritual being occupying physical space. And when I leave this planet, I will continue to be, just as I have always been.

When I write about the real "me," I am proclaiming my trust in a spiritual identity. As a created extension of God, when my body stops breathing I simply will move toward the Universal Love in a Divine merger.

There is no "religion" presented in these pages. Instead there is hope, love, trust, joy, and peace. Please don't theologically nit-pick. If you want to quibble, find someone who loves to debate. On the other hand, if you want to embrace Divine Love, open your arms and dance with the Spirit.

The music has been playing for a long time, already.

"My true identity is so secure,
so lofty, sinless, glorious, and great,
wholly loving and free from guilt,
that Heaven looks to It to give it light!"

A Course In Miracles, Lesson 224, P. 393

If I Should Wake Before I Die

Afterlife

Man says, "How is it possible,
when I am dead, that I shall be
brought forth alive?"
Does he not remember that
We have created him once,
and he was nothing then.

The Qur'an

If I Should Wake Before I Die

When it comes to Afterlife, science must fly out of the window.

Absolute proof is unavailable in the argument for Afterlife. When all is said and done, and it comes down to the final breath, you either believe in the ongoingness of life or you do not. That old word "faith" raises its powerful head here and makes noise for the continuity of your soul.

All of the major religions of the world point toward a "heaven" of some type. And they all have their systems and directions for getting there. Some call for a record keeping program which determines where you go and how high. Others speak of Karma or a recycling center which spins you back to try it again. Many imply some type of judgment by a higher court, deciding the next step in your journey.

Personally, I believe in a Re-union of Love.

Somewhere I read that we are not human beings trying to have a Spiritual experience but rather Spiritual beings having a human experience. As I see it, this means that we came to this planet as an extension of God, the Intentional Force of Love that maintains all of life.

The notion that you are an extension of God practicing your humanity may be new to you. I suspect, however, that it is not news to your soul, but rather very familiar. Dying becomes a human experience for your Spirit. And with your death, your Spirit, the core of your existence, re-unites with Love.

All the fear we endure in the dying process rests upon our inability to remember "who we are." You are not your body but rather an expression of the Love of God in human form. In a sense, your Spirit "uses" your body as a tool to haul it around until there is no longer any use for it.

Afterlife

Your Spirit putting your body "down," is what we call death.

Dying then, is the process of the separation between the Spirit and the body. We all go through it, and some manage easier than others. At best, death is a struggle as this separation occurs. And at worst, when release is reluctant, dying becomes coated with suffering.

There are those reading these words who will say, "I don't believe that." That's fine. No one forces us to believe anything about life after life.

For me, I choose to hold to the belief that I am an extension of God, a Spiritual being living within this frail and fragile body. When it is time for my transformation from this side to the other, I will lay my body down and soar toward the Love Force of the universe.

And as I attempt to understand the Unconditional Love of creation, I do not see judgment, punishment, or separation anywhere except in our own insanity. To view God as "keeping a list and checking it twice" is to confuse the Almighty with the ever watchful eyes of dad and mom.

As you read this in your dying process, I invite you to go inside yourself and speak to the Love Force within. Connect with your Spiritual self and draw upon the re-assurance that rests there. And in that connection, realize that you are part of the Loving Force we call God and therefore can NEVER be separated from Him.

Death then becomes a return to the familiar — a going home to your roots.

It clearly will be an incredible homecoming party, and the food will be great!

If I Should Wake Before I Die

WHAT THEY DO ABOVE

All we know
Of what they do above,
Is that they happy are,
And that they love.

Edmund Waller, 1645

UNION WITH GOD

The soul, passing out of itself by dying to itself
necessarily passed into its divine object.
This is the law of transition. When it passes
out of self, which is limited, and therefore
is not God, it necessarily passes into
the unlimited and universal, which is God.

Vaughan, *Theosophy*

RAISED TO LIFE

This is how it will be
when the dead are raised to life.
When the body is buried, it is mortal,
when raised it will be immortal.
When buried, it is ugly and weak;
when raised it will be beautiful and strong.
When buried, it is a physical body.
When raised, it will be a spiritual body.

I Corinthians 15:42-45

4

SELF IS EVERYWHERE

Self is everywhere shining forth from all beings,
vaster than the vast, subtler than the most
subtle, unreachable, yet nearer than breath,
than heartbeat.
Eye cannot see it, ear cannot hear it nor
tongue utter it; only in deep absorption
can the mind, grown pure and silent,
merge with the formless truth.
As soon as you find it, you are free;
you have found yourself;
you have solved the great riddle;
your heart forever is at peace.
Whole, you enter the Whole.
Your personal self returns to its
radiant, intimate, deathless source.

Upanishad

DISSOLVER OF SUGAR

Dissolver of sugar, dissolve me,
If this is the time.
Do it ever gently with a touch
of a hand, or a look,
Every morning I wait at dawn.
Or do it suddenly like an execution.
How else can I get ready for death?
You breathe without a body, like a spark.
You grieve, and I begin to feel lighter.
You keep me away with your arm,
but the keeping away is pulling me in.

Rumi,
Translation by Moyne and Barks

If I Should Wake Before I Die

Anger

Anger would
inflict punishment
on another,
meanwhile,
it tortures itself.

Publilius Syrus

If I Should Wake Before I Die

No matter how you slice it, anger is directly linked with loss.

Simply put, when you don't get your own way, anger pays a visit. You can give it all sorts of names such as disappointment, frustration, or just being upset. The bottom line, however, is that we all get angry when things don't go our way.

This probably roots in childhood during those times when we felt thwarted by the big people in life. Maybe it was something as simple as wanting to pet the cat, only to be yanked away by an over-protective parent. Or perhaps there was a time when you needed special attention, but your mother was overburdened with countless other tasks. Regardless of the logic or rationale behind these actions, you found yourself disappointed.

In all likelihood, you may have screamed or cried. Children do that.

Today, it's not so easy. You still get thwarted by the curve balls of life, but it's not as easy to recognize the pitcher. And just as when you were a child, anger needs to be expressed. However, because you are grown-up and mature doesn't mean you have any more of an idea how to express your anger than it did when you were a frustrated infant.

When your doctor told you to go home and get your affairs in order, nothing much was said about the potential rage festering inside. As your body betrays you in ways large and small, nothing is spoken of the feelings which emerge from this incredible loss. And as you consider the losses descending upon you, what is to be done with the countless emotions which erupt with each thought?

For most people, dying is a damnable experience.

Of course, there are those unusual persons for whom anger is a lifelong stranger. They have found

Anger

ways to keep it at a distance or to turn it into something productive or creative. Most of us are not that skilled. Dying people are usually angry because they are dying; and family members are angry because of the potential loss of someone they deeply love.

Given the fact that anger is an ongoing part of life and death, the question is what to do about all of this? Several years ago I attended a conference designed to help us do "anger work." This meant we pounded pillows with foam bats while screaming at the top of our lungs. Actually, even though my knees got brush-burned, it did help. Physical release can be important.

But not always possible. What do you do when you're lying in bed and your body is too weak to express your anger?

First of all, try to center yourself enough to identify what it is that you're really angry about. As the Course in Miracles says, "I am never upset for the reason I think." So begin the process of "peeling the onion" to get at the bottom of your hurt or injured feelings. Is it your disease or the fact that you're too young to die? Is it your pain or the thought of having to leave everyone you love? Is it something from your past that you have never been able to resolve, or is it that you hate the way your Aide incessantly talks?

Stephen Levine says that we are still angry over having to leave our mother's womb. Maybe that's so; I'm not certain. However, I do know that it is very important to recognize where your anger is rooted in order to cleanse yourself of whatever poison it feeds into your system.

Second, since most Hospice patients do not have the energy nor strength to pound pillows, or rant and rave, and to tell you the truth, those methods never did a lot to resolve deep hurt, a better way to release your anger needs to be found. Unfortunately, the ways in which you expressed anger in your past will probably be the methods you choose to express it now. Sadly, most of us never learned how to release our frustration and rage when we felt well, therefore, those ways won't work any better today.

Since physical release, for the most part, is probably impossible, the use of your mind becomes essential to help you work through your anger. And working through your anger does not mean mentally "getting even" with the source of your past hurts. Instead it calls for a brand new way of looking at your past, seeing things through the eyes of love and understanding instead of the "old way" of justifying your anger.

How many times have you lain awake at night, staring into the dark, with your mind going over the ways in which you have been wronged? Sadly, there is almost a pleasure that comes with deliciously licking your lips as you one more time play the role of the helpless victim. And while I wish we had time to debate together the litany of wrongs that have been inflicted on you, we don't.

The fact is that you are in the process of dying, and the need for releasing any and all grudges against the world is critical to your Transformation and inner healing. The truth of the matter is that most of us would rather be right than happy. Unfortunately, that can happen, but an enormous opportunity would be lost for you to release those anger-filled thoughts, which have followed you, sometimes over decades.

An important question to ask yourself at this time

is: would I like to release my thoughts and judgments of the past in order to transform my present journey? This is a huge question, and one that cannot be answered lightly. A "yes" answer means a willingness to unfasten your wagon from all the preconceived judgments of yesterday.

This means much more than "overlooking" what has been done to you, because even that position verifies the injuries that others have inflicted on you. Rather, releasing your judgments of the past means exactly that. It is a way of saying that you really don't have any idea what those past events meant.

Since you are never able to get inside the heart and mind of others, all of your thoughts about their treatment of you boils down to good old-fashioned guess-work. For example, a parent who treated you in a fashion which you perceived as "harsh," may have been following some kind of inter-generational programming from his or her parents in terms of raising children in a proper way. How can anyone know, even for a moment, what the deepest unresolved issues of parents might be?

So, I suppose the real question is: would you prefer to hold on to your ideas of what people did to you and why, or instead, embrace an open and compassionate view of any and all "injuries?" Holding on to the former means that you retain your anger, accepting the latter says that you choose love over hate. One will lead to inner healing and the other to stagnation.

It is your choice. I can tell you, however, that the path toward Transformation makes the dying journey more pleasant, as well as fills your room with a loving energy that you cannot imagine.

If I Should Wake Before I Die

A NEW WAY

…So get rid of your old self,
which made you live as you used to.
Your hearts and minds must be made
completely new, and you must put on
your new self, which is created in God's likeness,
and reveals itself in the true life
that is upright and Holy.

…If you become angry, do not let your anger
lead you into sin, and do not stay angry all day…

Do not use harmful words, but only helpful words,
the kind that build up
and provide what is needed,
so that what you say will do good
to those who hear you.

Ephesians 4:22-24, 29

THE THOUSAND WORDS

Better than a thousand useless words
Is one word which brings peace.
Better than a thousand useless verses
Is one line which brings joy.
Better than a thousand useless poems
Is one poem which brings love.

…'He abused me, he struck me,
he overcame me, he robbed me,' —
in those who harbor such thoughts
hatred will never cease.

'He abused me, he struck me,
he overcame me, he robbed me,' —
in those who do not harbor such thoughts
hatred will cease.

The Dhammapada

Anger

SOME DAY

Some day comes the Great Awakening
when we realize that this life
is no more than a dream.
Yet the foolish go on
thinking they are awake
surveying the panorama of life
with such clarity,
they call this one a prince
and that one a peasant —
What delusion!

Chuang Tzu

HOLINESS

The holiest spot on earth
is where an ancient hatred
has become a present love.

A Course In Miracles, Text, p. 522

MAKING PEACE

The recompense of an evil deed
is an evil like it,
so if anyone pardons and makes peace
it rests with God to reward him.

Koran

If I Should Wake Before I Die

Breathing

*And God
breathed
into Creation
the Breath of life.*

Genesis 2:7

If I Should Wake Before I Die

When my oldest son was born my grandmother expressed great distress over the cat that prowled the halls of our house. "That cat will steal the baby's breath," she warned me, insisting that the door to the baby's room be kept closed at all times.

I never knew that cats were breath stealers so I never worried about it. In fact, until I had a heart attack, I never worried about breath at all.

Now I think about it — considerably. And I suspect, so do you.

When you're facing death, the breath becomes a matter of enormous importance. It is, in fact, a prime necessity for life. In many of the world's religions, the breath is a reflection of the Divine spark placed in men and women, allowing for them to function with independence and freedom of choice.

From a purely physical point of view, breath is the stuff of life.

Therefore, being hungry for air is scary business. Regardless of how powerful your faith might be, when the body craves oxygen, fear enters in.

In the dying process, there are many different ways the body breaks down. Your skin can become compromised, your organs semi-productive, and your breath difficult. It is all a part of the process of leaving the body. In fact, until you finally let go of your breath, you will remain on this side of creation.

Losing your breath is a part of your Transformation. The fact that it is frightening is a given. But then, for most of us, dying is a fearful journey. It is a letting go of everything we have known. And this includes our breath.

Breathing

So what can you do to make it a little easier?

First of all, *remember* to breathe. Are you aware that when we become upset or frightened, there is a tendency to forget to breathe? Notice yourself when you are agitated. Are you breathing, or just holding your breath? Is it shallow instead of deep and full? Try to remember to calmly take full breaths.

Secondly, if you feel well enough, follow your breath up and down. Make it your focus as a part of meditation. Keep your mind following the flow of the air into your nose and down into the lungs. Next vision the breath filling your lungs and then allow it to exhale. Through it all, try to keep your focus on only the movement of your breath. In this way, your mind can release all distracting and fearful thoughts as you focus on the up and down movements of the breath.

Finally, remember that your breath came from God. It was a present to you at birth — can you recall that first gasp and wail? The spark of the Divine was given to you when you entered this world, and it can only be placed back in the hands of God when you leave. "The Lord giveth and the Lord taketh away," is not a warning. It is, instead, a promise of comfort.

When you die, it is a return to the familiar. Rather than a loss, from the Spiritual perspective it is a going home — the breath returning to the Breath.

CONNECTIONS

By air, as by a thread, this world
and all beings are strung together.
Breath is the life of all things.

Upanishad, III. 7,2

17

If I Should Wake Before I Die

CEASING OF BREATH

As a heavily loaded cart goes creaking,
just so this bodily self,
mounted by the intelligent Self,
goes groaning when one
is breathing one's last.
…As noblemen, policemen,
chariot-drivers and village heads
gather around a king
who is about to depart,
just so do all the breaths gather around the
soul at the end,
when one is breathing one's last.

Brihad-aranyaka Upanishad, 4:3

TO BE INSTRUMENTS OF GOD

A small wooden flute, an empty hollow reed,
rests in her silent hand.
It awaits the breath of one who creates song
through its open form.
My often-empty life rests in the hand of God;
like a hollowed flute, it yearns for the melody
which only Breath can give.
The small wooden flute and I,
we need the one who breathes,
we await the one who makes melody.
And the one whose touch creates,
awaits our empty, ordinary forms,
so that the song-starved world
may be fed with golden melodies.

Joyce Rupp,
May I Have This Dance?

Breathing

GOD'S BREATH

Even birds and animals
have much they could teach you,
ask the creatures of the sea
for their wisdom.
All of them know
the Lord's hand made them.
It is God who directs the lives
of His creatures;
every man's life is in His Breath.

Job 12:9,10

SINKING INTO WISDOM

When the breath has ceased,
the vital force will have sunk into
the nerve center of Wisdom,
and the Knower will experience
the Clear Light of the Natural Condition.

Tibetan Book of the Dead
(8th Century)

CLOSE TO GOD

Speak to Him thou for He hears
and Spirit with Spirit can meet —
Closer is He than breathing,
and nearer than hands and feet.

Alfred Tennyson

If I Should Wake Before I Die

Death

For ten minutes I was laughing
out of control as I saw that
part of my body is always dying.
What is there to fear?
Life and death are simultaneous:
2,500,000 red cells are being born
and consumed every second!
We are living flames, burning at the edge
of this incredible joy.

Michael Murphy, *Jacob Atabet*

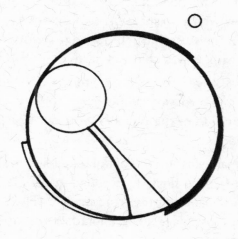

If I Should Wake Before I Die

When my grandfather died, his body was placed in a coffin in my grandmother's living room. I remember standing alone next to his body, an eight-year old boy with a normal sense of curiosity. When I mustered up enough courage, I touched his forehead. It was cold and hard.

Only six weeks earlier I had sat on the couch beside him tossing rubber rings toward a peg on the far side of the room. I won, but I suspect he allowed it.

The man lying in the coffin looked like my grandfather but the similarity stopped there. He smelled like lilacs and felt like cold marble. Even I knew, at that young age, my grandfather was not there; he was gone.

Countless funerals later, I still feel strange. Saying words over an empty shell is a struggle for me. Oh, I understand the psychological importance to the family, already overwhelmed by grief and loss, nevertheless, there is a powerful tendency to idolize an empty body.

We live in a culture emerged in body thinking; our views of death reflect such an obsession. When my father died, our family drove forty miles to purchase a perfect tie for his funeral outfit. I still chuckle as I recall spending more money on my father's funeral tie than he had ever spent on himself when alive. It was important, however, that he "look good."

Death, therefore, by definition becomes an enemy since the body appears to be the big-time loser in the match-up. And if I am "only a body," then it certainly makes sense to keep death at a healthy distance.

Death

Perhaps it is time for a more friendly view of death.

Dying is a process that we are all engaged in from the moment of birth. As you read these words, you are actively dying. The key here is to understand that dying is a movement toward Death.

There is a tendency, however, to view Death as an endpoint — an arrival, such as a railroad station or bus stop.

However, such a limited view of Death is neither helpful nor accurate. Rather than being viewed as a point in time, Death is better seen as a transforming, active movement in your life. It is a vessel which carries you from this side of life to the other.

Imagine your dying process somewhat like a journey to a wide river. When you arrive at the docks, your spirit (or soul) makes a decision to leave your body on this side of the river, choosing instead to cross over without all that excess body-baggage. Stepping out of your body, you board the ship for the next phase of your voyage.

Death is the passage from body life to spirit life. For decades your spirit has used your body to haul you around. At the moment of death, there is a release from all that body-baggage, pain, and struggle. As Emmanuel said, "Death is like taking off a tight shoe."

Often when I have driven into northeastern Pennsylvania, I have passed through the Lehigh Tunnel. Because of the surrounding mountains to the north, it is possible to enter the tunnel in a rain or snow storm, only to exit into bright sunlight. To me, this is a fine example of the death journey — from this side to the next.

Death is a passage from the heaviness of body to

If I Should Wake Before I Die

embracing the lightness of spirit. It is the only way to "get there from here." Equally, it is a time when you remember the real you, who entered your body at birth.

Indeed, death *is* an address change. For some, it is not a voluntary move; for others, it may be a welcome transition. Regardless it will happen to us all.

By the way, when you arrive on the other side of the river, there will be quite a crowd to greet you. Get ready for a grand party. And if you have trouble believing this, why not visualize it anyway. It can do wonders for your spirit and may carry you through one or two difficult nights.

NOTHING IS DEAD

*It is the secret of the world
that all things subsist and do not die,
but only retire a little from sight
and afterwards return again...
Nothing is dead; men feign themselves dead,
and endure mock funerals
and mournful Obituaries,
and there they stand looking out of the window,
sound and well, in some new and strange disguise.*

*Jesus is not dead; he is very alive: nor John,
nor Paul, nor Mahomet, nor Aristotle;
at times we believe we have seen them all, and
could easily tell the names
under which they go.*

Ralph Waldo Emerson

Death

MANY MANSIONS

"Do not be worried and upset,"
...Jesus told them.
"Believe in God and believe also in me.
There are many rooms in my Father's house,
and I am going to prepare a place for you.
I would not tell you this if it were not so.
And after I go and prepare
a place for you, I will come back
and take you to myself
so that you will be where I am."

John 14

A SWEET DEATH

The blue dot, which we call the Blue Pearl
dwells in the spiritual center, in the crown of
the head. It is the body of the Self.
All consciousness is contained in it.
All of the dynamism of the breathing process
comes from the Blue Pearl.

If a person dies very beautifully, the soul
can be seen departing in the Blue Pearl.

This is what great beings ask of God,
"O God, if You really want to give me something,
give me a good death, a sweet death."

Swami Muktananda

If I Should Wake Before I Die

DISSOLVING INTO GOD

"Please sir, instruct me further."
"So be it, my son. Put this salt in the water
and come back tomorrow."

Svetaketu did so and returned the next morning.

His father said, "Please return to me the salt
you placed in the water yesterday."

Svetaketu looked but could not find it.

"But sir, all the salt has dissolved."
"How does the water at the top taste?"
"Like salt."
"And at the middle?"
"Like salt."
"And at the bottom."
"Like salt."

"My son, the salt remains in the water
even though you do not see it; and though
you do not see that Pure Being,
He is fully present in you and everywhere else.
That One alone is the essence of all, the soul
of the world, and You are That! You are That!"

Upanishads

LAUGHING

Everyone is so afraid of death,
but the real sufis just laugh:
nothing tyrannizes their hearts.
What strikes the oyster shell
doesn't damage the pearl.

Rumi

Dignity

Our dignity is not in what we do,
but in what we understand.

George Santayana

If I Should Wake Before I Die

At times, dying can be quite undignified.

Diapers, bed pans, and someone you hardly know bathing your bottom, can quickly wash away your sense of self-esteem. It's hard to feel very stately when your humanity pokes through with such compelling force.

Loss of control is a familiar bed-fellow with the dying process. For most of us, uncontrollable situations are the very things we have spent a great deal of time trying to avoid. Historically, our lives have been cluttered with attempts to maintain some fantasies of power and control. The fact is that even when we feel well, few of us cope decently with the uncontrollable.

If during my normal living experiences, I have equated "being in control" with the finer way of life, I will almost immediately get into trouble when I actively enter the dying process. Dying is God's way of reminding us that our feeble attempts at control are only illusions of the grandest kind.

Often patients will say to me, "I just want to maintain my dignity."

So do I, but I'm not really sure what that means. My suspicions say that they're talking about dying "cleanly." This is sort of another way of saying that a dignified death is an unmessy death.

The truth of the matter is that most dying is dirty business. Just the concept of dying is a statement of loss of control. The most capable people still die. CEO's and priests die, as do homemakers and kids. Cancer dances circumstantially through families and neighborhoods striking here and there on an apparent whim. And through it all, we have little control over how long we linger or how quickly we leave.

If you feel that weak bladder control or the inability to feed yourself is a negation of your dignity, you're

Dignity

in trouble right now. These things, and countless other physical and emotional limitations are a normal part of dying. Whether you mess yourself or manage to make it to the commode has nothing to do with your worth.

And self-worth is what dignity is all about.

Dignity comes from the Latin and means "worthy." It clearly points to your sense of "self" and has nothing to do with what others think. Dignity is a self-concept, not a judgment of others, or an opinion of a neighbor.

Dying with dignity means you graciously accept the daily things that happen to your body — that you understand that body-breakdown is a normal and natural part of the spirit leaving. You have dignity when you accept your humanity, and all the possible ruptures or craziness that can happen to you.

Does it make you any less a person if someone has to clean up after you? Are you less dignified if you weep through the night? If you spit up your lunch on the clean sheets, does that mean something is wrong with you? If you and your son have reversed roles, and now he has to change your diaper, have you let him down?

Only if you believe it.

Dying with dignity is accepting your body as the weak, unpredictable tool that it is. Some bodies last fifty years, and some eighty, but eventually, they all break down and fall to pieces. And often it's messy. It is a truth of the human condition.

The issue is not whether you like it — no one does. Rather, it is whether you can graciously surrender to the truth.

A death with dignity is one in which you cough, spit, wet, and love yourself straight through from this side to the next.

If I Should Wake Before I Die

YOUR LIFE AS A GIFT

Whether it pleases us or not,
each moment is a gift.
No matter how unpleasant the wrapping,
inside is something wonderful
that life wants to give us.
It we let it pass without opening it,
we have missed something priceless.

Polly Berrien Berends

LIVING IN YOU

Know, then, Who abides with you merely
by recognizing what is there already,
and do not be satisfied with imaginary
comforters, for the Comforter of God is in you.

Course In Miracles, Ch. 11, P. 184

OUT OF NOTHING

God creates out of nothing.
Therefore, until a man is nothing,
God can make nothing out of him.

Martin Luther

PERFECTION

These roses under my window
make no reference
to former roses or to better ones.
They are what they are;
they exist with God today.
There is no time to them.
There is simply the rose.
It is perfect in every moment of its existence.

Ralph Waldo Emerson

Dignity

COME TO GOD

Come, come, whoever you are
Wanderer, worshipper, lover of leaving —
It doesn't matter.
Ours is not a caravan of despair.
Come, even if you have broken your vow
a hundred times, ten thousand times —
Come, come again, come.

Rumi

GOD WANTS YOU!

God does not ask your ability
or your inability.
He asks only your availability.

Mary Kay Ash

OUT OF BROKENNESS

There is a brokenness out of which
comes the unbroken, a shatteredness
out of which blooms the unshatterable.
There is a sorrow beyond all grief
which leads to joy, and a fragility
out of whose depths emerges strength.

There is a hollow space too vast for words
through which we pass with each loss,
out of whose darkness
we are sanctioned into being
There is a cry deeper than all sound
whose serrated edges cut the heart
as we break open to the place inside
which is unbreakable and whole,
while learning to sing.

Rashani

If I Should Wake Before I Die

Doubt

O Lord, if there is a Lord,
Save my soul, if I have a soul.

Ernest Renan, *Prayer of a Skeptic*

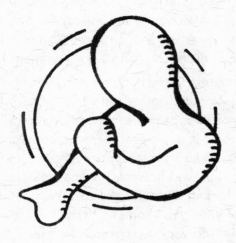

If I Should Wake Before I Die

Doubt, it seems to me, is a fact of life. I know that in my lifetime I have doubted the wisdom of teachers and the dedication of preachers. I have certainly doubted my elected officials, as well as some of the folks hired to enforce the rules of the land. And I remember doubting my Sunday School teachers when they talked about a loving God who required blood in order to right a wrong relationship.

My grandmother had trouble with my doubts, citing various chapters and verses which warned of the hot fires of hell for those doubters like me. I remember emotional sermons, punctuated with outstretched arms meant to represent Jesus on the cross, but which were designed to caution any doubters in the audience to take a good lesson from "doubting Thomas." "You don't want to be like him, do you," suggested my grandmother.

The problem for me was that I understood Thomas.

He seemed to raise practical issues that needed to be heard. It's very hard not to wonder about life, death, and God, if you even allow your mind to question anything at all. There were a lot of things I never understood, and still don't, that I have doubts about.

My guess is that you, also, have doubted many things in your lifetime. Probably in the past few months you may have wondered if the medical profession knew what it was doing in regards to your own physical condition. In retrospect, you may be doubting the wisdom of some of the decisions you have made for yourself. It seems to me that doubt is only natural at times of great difficulties in our lives.

Sometimes there are doubting personalities — those persons who question from the beginning. Perhaps you are one of those individuals, who during the normal course of your life, tried to examine and

Doubt

look at all sides of an issue. While this can be seen as a positive attribute, it is also true that asking too many questions can hold you back from forward movement in your life. On the other hand, ignoring the many sides of a problem can lead to a limited solution. My guess is, however, that doubt is a positive feeling, and only turns into trouble when it gets mixed with fear, that old dragon we all face. Back in the early 1800's, Julis and August Hare, two English clerics, wrote, "Half the failures of the world arise from pulling in one's horse as he is leaping." When the horse lands on its back because we have yanked on the reins in midair, this is the result of mixing doubt with fear.

It is almost certain that doubt will enter as a part of the dying process. I recall visiting an 82 year old woman, dying of ovarian cancer. She had been an active and vital church member her entire life.

When she called to ask me to visit, I was surprised since she received daily visits from her pastor. "I wanted to talk with you," she said, "about my doubts. And I was afraid to speak to my own pastor about them because he would have been ashamed of me." She rested silently in her hospital bed for a few minutes before continuing, "Do you think that I am worthy of God, and do you think there really is a heaven and an afterlife?"

In that question, I believe this woman was raising the common ground explored by all dying people. Are the beliefs of childhood, and the teachings that have been accepted throughout my life really true? And, of course, there is no more difficult time to ask that question than in the midst of actively dying. Fear is so strong and powerful during the final months of life that doubt can easily grow to monstrous proportions.

If I Should Wake Before I Die

It is not unusual to discover patients, who have been incredibly faithful to their religious beliefs, and at the same time racing all over the landscape with questions and doubts. Is there really a God? Does He care about me at all? Is there life after death, and is it for me? Add to these questions the element of the physical and emotional pain commonly experienced by dying people, and it is no wonder that doubts flow everywhere.

So, what do I have to say to you about your doubts? Well, first of all, don't worry about them. Whether you doubt God, or His love, does not change or influence God and His love one iota. Your doubts are simply your doubts. God is God, and His love is ever flowing, whether you accept it, doubt it, or reject it. In this case, you can't, and won't lose.

Now, obviously, the more you are able to trust in those beliefs which have always (or sometimes) brought you peace and comfort, the more at ease you will be in your dying process. Since trust is the opposite of doubt, the more you are able to trust your inner "knowing" about God and His love, the easier life will become for you in the peace department. This means that is it important for you to turn to your inner "guide" or "knowing" in order to feel more at rest during these days.

Some folks, and this may be your case, have trouble, however, even believing in their inner guide, another doubting difficulty. If this is so, can you remember back to a time when your "intuition" helped you know something in life? Maybe it was something so simple as thinking about a friend and suddenly having the telephone ring, only to pick up the receiver to his or her voice. Or perhaps you just "knew" you were going to get a certain job, or have a child, or live in a special house. These are all

Doubt

examples of the inner voice, which is still available to you. Now, I know that some of you will call these examples coincidences. Someone has written that a coincidence is a "miracle in which God has chosen to remain anonymous." Regardless of how you view this, whatever you are able to hold on to which will connect you more deeply with the core of Trust inside, will provide more inner comfort and serenity.

Sometimes, when trust has disappeared and doubt is mixed with fear, doing a number on your ability to rest or sleep, you may find that holding on to something tangible can be helpful. Find something among your possessions that has special meaning to you, and hold it in the palm of your hand. Squeeze it, sleep with it, place it against your chest, and feel the solidness of the object. It may be something as simple as a small stone which you found in your back yard, or a piece of jewelry given to you by someone you love. For some of you, holding on to the Rosary gives you a sense of the Trusting force in life. You might want to try a small piece of smooth wood, or a polished piece of glass.

Holding on to the tangible can easily point the way to the ultimate Intangible in life — the power and love of God. It is easy, at times, to doubt your life-long beliefs. Fear does that to all of us, at one time or another. Holding on to something solid, that carries special symbolic meaning, can be the way through the door of doubt to the place of rest and trust.

There is a song out these days called *"There is No Solid Ground."* No one should have to interpret that song for you since we have all discovered that sooner or later, the very ground on which we walk seems to collapse. We live in a world where there is no safety, regardless of how much we try to make

If I Should Wake Before I Die

it safe. No wonder, then, that we doubt. All we can hold to is the strength of our beliefs. And sometimes those lifelong beliefs seem to fade in the darkness of doubt. However, as Mary Bardiner Brainard said in *Not Known*, "I would rather work with God in the dark, than go alone in the light."

So grab on to something solid, close you eyes, and trust with all your might. When you step out, there will be Solid Ground to hold you. That's a promise.

QUESTION

Question with boldness even the existence
of God; because, if there be one he must
more approve of the homage of reason,
than that of blindfolded fear.

Thomas Jefferson, 1787

THE UNKNOWN GOD

As I passed by, and beheld your devotions,
I found an altar with this inscription:
TO AN UNKNOWN GOD.

The apostle Paul: Acts 17

THE PROPERNESS OF DOUBT

It is proper to doubt.
Do not be lead by holy scriptures,
or by mere logic or inference,
or by appearances, or by the authority
of religious teachers. But when you realize
that something is unwholesome and bad for you,
give it up. And when you realize that some-
thing is wholesome and good for you, do it.

The Buddha

Doubt

FAITH AND FAITHLESSNESS

*It cannot be difficult to realize that faith must
be the opposite of faithlessness. Yet the difference
in how they operate is less apparent, though it
follows directly from the fundamental difference
in what they are. Faithlessness would always
limit and attack; faith would remove all
limitations and make whole. Faithlessness
would interpose illusions between the Son
(child) of God and his Creator; faith would
remove all obstacles that seem to raise
between them. Faithlessness is wholly dedicated
to illusions; faith wholly to truth. Partial
dedication is impossible. Truth is the absence
of illusion; illusion the absence of truth.
Both cannot be together, nor perceived in
the same place. To dedicate yourself to both
is to set up a goal forever impossible to attain,
for part of it is sought through the body, thought
of as a means for seeking out reality through
attack . The other part would heal, and therefore calls upon the mind and not the body.*

Course in Miracles, Ch. 19, P. 372

THE LEDGE

*There I was on a ledge,
lookin' over the edge
Feelin' like the face of a clown,
I said to God,
"I gotta know before I jump, what's below?"
He said, "I'll tell you on the way down..."*

Brit Lay, *Surrender*

If I Should Wake Before I Die

THE EDGE

When you come to the edge
of all that you know,
you must believe one of two things;
There will be earth to stand on,
or you will be given wings to fly.

Source Unknown

HOPED FOR

Faith is the substance
of things hoped for,
the evidence of things
not seen.

Hebrews 11:1

LET GO

Let go the things in which
you are in doubt,
for the things in which
there is no doubt.

Mohammed

Eating

They shall hunger no more.

Revelation 7:16

If I Should Wake Before I Die

Eating is an active part of life. Not eating is a normal part of dying. The problem is that other folks have a lot of difficulty with your loss of appetite. Probably they hook up your half-eaten sandwich with one day closer to your change of address. And they may be right. My doctor friend tells me that a large percentage of what you eat goes to feed your tumor. So, if you have cancer and don't eat, there's some solace in the thought that your tumor isn't getting any chubbier from chocolate cake. Of course, it still will grow but maybe you're not actively nursing it.

You know better than anyone else that the reason you're not eating is simply because you're not hungry. When you don't have an appetite, it's tough to force food into your mouth, no matter how tasty it may be. In fact, just the odor of some of your favorite foods may now nauseate you.

Eating and hunger go hand in hand. So, the best rule of thumb that I know is: if you're not hungry, don't eat. On the other hand, when your stomach calls for something to eat, go for it! And try not to let others push you too much in one direction or the other.

Another thought about all of this has to do with the real meaning of hunger. It seems to me that many of us spend a great deal of our lives trying to fill a void that we have carried with us since birth. There is a part of us that is never satisfied, no matter how well life may go. It is almost as if there is a "hunger" beyond the physical.

Pizza or ice cream may taste good, and you can certainly eat enough to fill your belly, however, it doesn't seem to touch that empty spot that always lets you know it's still hungry. The Buddhists talk about the search that we all are born into, namely,

Eating

the hunting for God. They also suggest that most of us end up looking for the right thing in the wrong place. Jesus puts it in terms of a "thirst" that goes unsatisfied because we have a need for "living water." This is a way of saying that there is never anything of a physical nature that will satisfy the spiritual craving we all have. At this point in the game of life, you are apt to be far more content with the feeding of your soul than your body. Soup and a piece of fruit will nourish your body, and if you're one of the fortunate ones to retain your appetite, you'll be hungry again within hours.

Prayer, meditation, and contemplation, however, will bring a lasting peace to your soul. It is another kind of food which has great implications for everyone since it is the only nourishment which lasts. If your stomach is upset, ask someone close to you to read you one of your favorite poems. Or turn on your tape player to a great piece of music. Invite a friend to rent a meaningful movie to touch your soul; then watch it together. These things are real "bread," the stuff of life.

So, the next time someone says, "What do you want to eat?" try this answer: "Give me a piece of a great symphony and a cup of inspirational poetry." It'll be a banquet unlike any you've ever had.

If I Should Wake Before I Die

THE CRAVINGS ARE STILLED

Two birds, one of them mortal,
the other immortal, live in the same tree.
The first one pecks at the fruit, sweet or bitter;
the second looks on without eating.
Thus the personal self pecks at the truth
of this world, bewildered by suffering,
always hungry for more.
But when he meets the True Self,
the resplendent God, the source of creation,
all his cravings are stilled.
Perceiving Self in all creatures,
he forgets himself in the service of all;
good and evil both vanish; delighting in Self,
playing like a child with Self, he does whatever
is called for, whatever the result.

The Upanishads

BEING FULL IN CHRIST

So let no one make rules about what you eat
or drink or about holy days or the New Moon
Festival or the Sabbath. All such things are
only a shadow of things in the future,
the reality is Christ…
Under Christ's control the whole body
is nourished and held together by
its joints and ligaments, and it grows
as God wants it to grow.

Colossians: 2:16,17,19

Eating

THE HUNGER FOR GOD

As the deer longs for flowing streams,
so my soul longs for you, O God.
I thirst for the living God;
I ache for Him day and night.
When will He fill me with his presence?
When will I see his face.
Why are you desolate, my soul?
Why weighed down by despair?
Trust in God; He will save you;
you will sing to Him with great joy.
My soul is heavy with anguish;
my heart keeps longing for God.
I am lost in a sea of wretchedness;
I drown in the waters of despair
The roar of waterfalls surround me,
and the waves crash over my head.

Why are you desolate, my soul?
Why weighed down by despair
Trust in God; He will save you,
you will sing to Him with great joy.

Psalm 42,
translated by Stephen Mitchell

If I Should Wake Before I Die

THOUGHTS WHILE EATING

With the first taste,
I promise to practice loving kindness.
With the second,
I promise to relieve the suffering of others.
With the third, I promise
to see the others' joy as my own.
With the fourth,
I promise to learn the way of
nonattachment and equanimity.

from *One Hundred Graces*
Marcia & Jack Kelly

FOOD FOR THE SOUL

I heard Thy voice from on high crying unto me,
"I am the Food of the full-grown: grow, and then
thou shalt feed on Me. Nor shalt thou change
Me into thy substance as thou changest the
food of thy flesh, but thou shalt be changed
into Mind."

Augustine, *Confessions*

Faith

Onward in faith —

and leave the rest to Heaven.

Robert Southey

If I Should Wake Before I Die

Faith is trusting that ultimately everything will be all right. It is believing that the arms of Love will hold you when everyone else has had to let go.

Such faith does not come from what you intellectually know, but rather it emerges from a profound assurance in a Power beyond yourself. And either you hold on to the belief or you do not. There is no grey area in faith.

Dying is an experience in a thousand tiny losses. From the betrayal of the muscles of the body to the gradual disappearance of energy, you feel the slippage of the familiar. That which you could count on yesterday you may not trust tomorrow.

Sometimes friends who don't know how to handle your illness find themselves unsure how to relate with you. There are some family members who fear your loss so much they seem distant, even when holding your hand. Even doctors often "release" you when faced with their own helplessness.

It's not easy to hold on to much when you're dying.

Most important, then, is the clinging to your faith in the protection and presence of God. Since the Spirit of God lives within, there is never a breath or sigh separate from Him. Loneliness and fear are not apart from His awareness.

Faith, then, is a statement of unity and connection. It is a belief in the joining of your spirit with the Highest Spirit, in which there is no separation.

This union is constant whether you believe it or not. Faith is the embracing of the inner-marriage between you and your Creator. It rests in your heart and not your head. Trying to "figure out" your faith is like blowing up a balloon with a hole in it. You can huff, puff, and blow until you're blue in the face, but the balloon will remain a limp piece of latex in your hand.

Faith

It is possible, of course, to put your faith in anything. You can have faith in your pain medication or the advice of your doctor. Every time you push the button on your remote control, you have faith in the signal between the control and your TV. When your kids say they'll call, you can put your faith in the belief that they mean what they say.

Eventually, however, faith in everything but the eternal falls aside. Through much of our lives we place our trust in things, people, and performance. The dying process pushes much of that trust aside since ultimately, you go through the final doorway without any visible help. In general, you die alone regardless of how many people are holding your hand or stroking your face.

Therefore, it is in dying that the faith in the timeless and limitless presence of God means the most. In that belief is the understanding that you do **NOT** walk through the doorway alone, but instead are carried on the shoulders of total Love.

True faith can be given meaning during the dying process itself. Letting go of trust in this world and grabbing on to faith in the eternal is a holy part of that process.

Hang on, and if the ride gets bumpy, hold tight.

THINGS HOPED FOR

*Faith is the substance
of things hoped for,
the evidence
of things not seen.*

Hebrews 11:1

If I Should Wake Before I Die

CONFIDENT ASSURANCE

Faith is a living
and unshakable confidence,
a belief in the grace of God
so assured that a man would die
a thousand deaths for its sake.

Martin Luther

CERTAINTY

I never saw a Moor
I never saw the Sea —
Yet know I how the Heather looks
And what a Billow be.
I never spoke with God
Nor visited in Heaven —
Yet certain am I of the spot
As if the Checks were given.

Emily Dickinson

RESTING IN GOD

I rest in God.
Completely undismayed, this thought
will carry you through storms and strife
past misery and pain, past loss and death,
and onward to the certainty of God.

As you close your eyes, sink into stillness.
Let these periods of rest and respite
reassure your mind that all its frantic fantasies
were but the dreams of fever
that has passed away.
Let it be still
and thankfully accept its healing.
No more fearful dreams will come,
now that you rest in God.

A Course in Miracles, Lesson 109

THE BREATH WITHIN YOU

Are you looking for Me?
I am in the next seat.
My shoulder is against yours.

You will not find Me in stupas,
not in Indian shrine rooms,
not in synagogues, nor in cathedrals.
not in masses, nor kirtans,
not in legs winding around your neck,
nor in eating nothing but vegetables.

When you really look for Me,
you will see Me instantly —
you will find Me in the tiniest house of time.
Kabir says: Student tell me what is God?
He is the breath inside the breath.

        Kabir

GREAT FAITH

Great faith is not the faith
that walks always in the light
and knows no darkness,
but the faith that perseveres
in spite of God's seeming silences,
and that faith will most certainly
and surely get its reward.

        Fr. Andrew SDC

If I Should Wake Before I Die

Fear

*For it is not death and pain
that is a fearful thing,
but the fear of death and pain.*

Epictetus

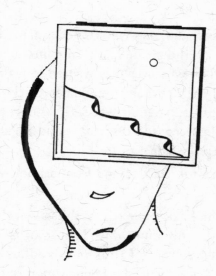

If I Should Wake Before I Die

When I was a child, walking to school each day, there was one thing I was afraid of... I called them the "big kids."

They were the ones who could harm me, knock my books on the ground, push me into a tree, or in general do whatever they wanted to with me. As I turned each corner, I remember quickly scanning the block to see if it was safe. Wherever it was possible, I crossed the street and walked where they usually didn't go.

In short, the walk to and from school was a daily dread.

Looking back on it today, there were probably fewer than five times when I got "caught" by the big kids. And most of those I talked my way into safety. Nevertheless, my anticipation of something bad happening controlled many of my thoughts, resulting in a campaign of strategies simply to walk across town.

For the most part, fear is like that. It fills our minds with the anticipation of the terrible, and reaches back from the future to contaminate the present. Fear is almost always pointing toward a future event or circumstance, surrounding it with clouds of the unknown.

Patients tell me of the "possibility of pain so great and terrible that I won't be able to stand it. And yet there is no choice except to stand it. But, what if I can't?" This thought, and others like it, gobble at people during the night.

Fear tends to ride herd over the mind in the dark. Palms grow sweaty and breath is sometimes hard to come by; sleep next to impossible. And, for the most part, it does all of its dirty work in the mind.

Fear

Indeed, fear is a matter of the mind's thought patterns.

When I used to have bad dreams during the night, my father would tell me to "think of something else." I suppose that was sound advice, but almost impossible to do when the demons were still crawling across the wallpaper in the corner of my bedroom.

With fear, the mind is almost always the primary culprit. My fear of the "big kids" did far more damage to me than the kids themselves. The thoughts I had of their cruelty carried more power than fifty big kids.

When you're spinning your fearful thoughts during the night, you are doing a major number on yourself. The anticipation of terrible things yet to come in itself is a form of self cruelty.

Fearful thinking, however, is a normal and natural part of our humanity. When you are dying, fear is going to be present. Regardless of your faith or trust in God, it is a given. When pain is surging through your organs, or if every breath is hard work, the body is going to be in a state of fear. For the most part, fear will accompany these instances, and short of learning to meditate in the midst of pain, you will simply have to endure those moments until they pass. And they will.

It is one thing to be consumed by fear in the midst of a panic attack, it is quite another to allow panic to run rampant through your mind in anticipation of future attacks. The anxiety in itself can bring such episodes to reality. Thinking fearful thoughts is rarely helpful to you in any way. They will not prevent your disease from proceeding, nor will they keep you safe.

If I Should Wake Before I Die

The sad truth of the matter is that your body is not safe. Vulnerability is a condition of birth. Thinking fearful thoughts about what might happen will not prevent anything.

There is no safety in life, instead there is only the possibility of peace.

The goal for all of us, then, is to learn to replace fearful thoughts with peace. Being cradled in the arms of God is a vision of inner peace. Recalling your physical vulnerability the next time you feel pain in your stomach simply feeds your fear demons. Although such thinking is very human, it is time for you to find another way.

Which would you prefer: to feel inner peace or terror?

The next time you find your mind reeling with fear, try to imagine yourself in a wonderful setting. It may be in a beautiful meadow, or standing by the sea.

Regardless of the place, find a spot in your mind where you feel at peace. When the fear enters your mind, gently push it aside and travel to your peace-filled place. Breathe as easily as you can and invite thoughts into your mind which bring you joy.

In one of John's letter to the early church, he writes that "perfect love casts out fear." It is a fact of life that you can't think two thoughts at the same time. So why not "cast" out the fear by thinking thoughts which bring you peace and joy?

Fear is a natural part of dying, but it does not have to occupy center stage. In this instance, since this is *your* life, you are the main actor as well as the director. Perhaps you could move the "big kids" to stage-right, and bring peace and sunlight to the center.

It *is* your choice.

FACING LIFE

We are not here just to survive
and live long...
We are here to live and know life
in its multi-dimensions,
to know life in its richness, in all its variety.

And when a man lives multi-dimensionally,
explores all possibilities available,
never shrinks back from any challenge,
goes, rushes to it, welcomes it,
rises to the occasion,
then life becomes a flame,
life blooms.

Bhagwan Shress Rajneesh,
The Sacred Yes

YOU HAVE NO IDEA

Eye has not seen, Ear has not heard,
Nor has it so much as dawned on man
What God has prepared for those who love Him.

I Corinthians 2:9

IF YOU ONLY KNEW

If you know Who walks beside you,
on the way that you have chosen,
fear would be impossible.

A Course in Miracles, Ch. 18, P. 353

THE CUP OF TREMBLING

Behold, I have taken out of thine hand
the cup of trembling...
thou shalt no more drink it again.

Isaiah 51:22

If I Should Wake Before I Die

FINDING COMFORT

Wanting to know God
is the road that leads to God,
and it is an easy road to travel.
God will come to meet you everywhere, he will
appear to you everywhere,
at times and places when you don't expect it,
while you are awake and while you are asleep,
while you are traveling and while you are at
home, while you are speaking and while you
are silent; for there is nothing
in which God does not exist.

The Hermetic Writings,
from *The Enlightened Mind*

CRYING OUT

"I cry out with my whole heart —
answer me, O Lord.
Save me from this ocean of darkness,
Show me a way out.
I rise before dawn and wait to hear your voice.
My eyes stay open past the midnight watch,
so that I might come to know all
you have taught me.

You are so near my Lord;
You are the eternal support;
You are the supreme goal...
I have but one prayer:
that every step I take be a step toward you."

Psalm 119 (partial)

Forgiveness

When you bury a mad dog,
don't leave his tail
above the ground.

Author Unknown

If I Should Wake Before I Die

Forgiveness occupies the center ring in the circus of life.

Childhood is risky business and by the time you reach adulthood, injuries have been rampant. Some are more severe than others but no one escapes the damages of parents, teachers, friends, and enemies. Life is a costly journey, and the wounding is often enormous.

Most of us, by the time we reach the final twists of our adventure, are in pain from the past. And if we are somewhat normal, we probably have kept score. Some people I know even jot down their hurts so they won't forget them. Keeping track of the villains in your life helps you know when it's safe to turn your back.

During the process of dying, past reflections are common. Lying in bed for hours at a time can lead to much "think time," during which old hurts and wounds soar into the present from the past. Previous grudges often resurface and the old feeling of being a victim can re-emerge.

A common phrase used in the middle of all of this is termed "cleaning up old business." This is another way of saying there is a need for "forgiveness" in your life. But letting go of the perceived injuries of the past is difficult work, especially when those wounds seem so clear in your mind and heart.

The plain fact is, however, that holding on to judgments and conclusions about yesterday may contaminate today. Joy and inner peace are hard to come by when old stuff smells up the present. It can even get in the way of your pain medication. Tumor pain combined with past resentments make the work of your morphine twice as difficult.

Forgiveness

My suspicion is that most everyone agrees that forgiveness is critical; the question seems to be — "Do you want to forgive?" Some people have held on to their judgments and conclusions of the past for so long that letting go would appear to diminish the importance of previous wounds.

Perhaps today is the time to change such thinking. True forgiveness can release you from so much old garbage that you cannot even imagine the peace and tranquility that can be experienced.

Two things are required.

First is the desire to forgive; second is the willingness to "see" differently.

You acquire desire by recognizing that you may have an attitude problem. Most of us do, and keeping score of past injuries is all the evidence you need. When someone said, "Don't forget where you bury the hatchet," they were not pointing toward forgiveness. The spouse who forgave a mate and then said, "I have forgiven and forgotten, but I don't want you to forget that I have forgiven and forgotten," hasn't really forgiven at all.

Do you wish to forgive your judgments of the past? If not, then hold on tight and kick and scream through to the end. You have that right.

My sense is that it will "cost" you dearly, however. Not in terms of punishment or eternal judgment, but rather in the tragedy of dying without peace. There is a great deal more to dying peacefully than simply the lack of physical pain. No one needs to tell you that however, because I suspect that's something you already know.

The desire to forgive is simply the willingness to shift from clenched fists to open hands.

"Seeing it differently," takes a bit more effort, however. It suggests that the judgments you have put on the perceived injuries of the past have created a "filtering" system over your eyes, so that you glance backwards through colored lenses. If each time you examine a past wound looking through the same colored glasses, you will "see" the same pain and arrive at identical conclusions.

"Seeing it differently" means looking through another window at the past. Abuse at the hands of an angry parent can lead to judgments about personal self-worth, as well as hatred toward the abuser. Looking through another glass — the window of grace — can help you see the fear-filled history of your parents. Perhaps they were raised in injury themselves, or they operated out of some level of terror.

Looking at others as you would imagine God looking at them is very helpful when trying to "see differently." Are you willing to look through the eyes of love instead of the glass of judgment? The willingness to see differently actually carries more power for inner peace than the results.

Letting go of old judgments and harsh conclusions can usher in joy in a way that you have never experienced it before. Replacing anger and hatred with love leads to enormous feelings of release. From a selfish standpoint, it serves you well to let go of those pains which may have haunted you for decades. Why not allow for an inner healing in this critical area?

Your soul will rejoice in gratitude.

Forgiveness

AN INSTRUMENT OF PEACE

Lord, make me an instrument of your peace,
Where there is hatred, let me sow love;
Where there is injury, pardon;
Where there is doubt, faith;
Where there is despair, hope;
Where there is darkness, light;
Where there is sadness, joy.

O Divine master,
Grant that I may not so much seek
To be consoled as to console,
To be understood as to understand,
To be loved as to love;
For it is in giving that we receive,
it is in pardoning that we are pardoned,
and it is in dying that we are born to eternal life.

St. Francis of Assisi

WHAT DO YOU WANT?

What could you want forgiveness can not give?
Do you want peace? Forgiveness offers it.
Do you want happiness, a quiet mind,
a certainty of purpose, and a sense of worth
and beauty that transcends the world?
Do you want care and safety
and the warmth of sure protection always?
Do you want a quietness
that cannot be disturbed, a gentleness that
never can be hurt, a deep abiding comfort,
and a rest so perfect it can never be upset?
All this Forgiveness offers you.

Forgiveness is the key to happiness.

A Course in Miracles, Lesson 122

If I Should Wake Before I Die

THE HIGHER WAY

Do not use harmful words,
but only helpful words,
the kind that build up and provide
what is needed, so that what you say
will do good to those who hear you.

And do not make God's spirit sad,
for the Spirit of God is God's mark
of ownership on you, a guarantee that
the Day will come when God will set you free.
Get rid of bitterness, passion, and anger.
No more shouting or insults,
No more hateful feelings of any sort.

Instead, be kind and tender-hearted toward
one another, and forgive one another
as God has forgiven you through Christ.

Ephesians 4:29-32

LOVE AND FORGIVENESS

There is no difficulty
that enough love will not conquer;
no disease that enough love will not heal;
no door that enough love will not open;
no guilt that enough love will not bridge;
no wall that enough love will not throw down;
no sin that enough love will not redeem.

It makes no difference how deeply muddled
the tangle, how great the mistake;
a sufficient realization of love will dissolve it all.

Emmet Fox

Friendship

It is one of the blessings
of old friends
that you can afford
to be stupid with them.

Ralph Waldo Emerson

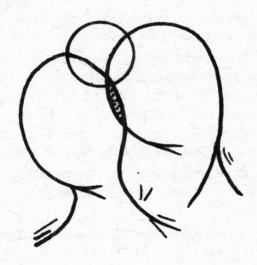

If I Should Wake Before I Die

Hugh Kingsmill quoted Michael Holroyd when he said, "Friends are God's apology for relatives." I like that quote and it reminded me of the time I attended a workshop where the speaker talked about our "families of choice." He implied that most of us in the room had been damaged in one way or another by our parents, siblings, and other well meaning family folks. "Sometimes," he said, "when you grow up, you may receive better support and encouragement from your friends than from your families. I call these friends my family of choice." He talked about some people who have photographs around their house of good friends rather than family members.

Good friends often enter your mind during the dying process. Memories are a part of spinning the old stories, some of which go all the way back to childhood. I have visited many hospice patients who have told me stories of old friends coming to see them, some traveling thousands of miles to say good-by. One patient, an old retired naval officer, told me that he sometimes received two or three telephone calls a day from his old Navy buddies. "They make my day," he said to me with a huge smile on his face.

A very hard part of dying is learning how to say good-by. Few of us are practiced at it since we have spent so much of our lives trying to learn how **NOT** to feel the pain of loss. Saying good-by to family members is tough work, and I'm not exactly sure how you do it. I do know there aren't any rights or wrongs about it, and most people stumble through somehow or other. Saying good-by to friends is something that few people attempt at all. Perhaps this is because they are often not around during the final months of life.

Friendship

But it doesn't have to be like that. Aristotle wrote, "What is a friend? A single soul in two bodies." For many of you this is a true statement since friendships have been an extremely vital and important part of your life. And what a gift it could be to you, and your friends, if they could also be a part of your dying process.

In listening to many patients over the years, I have discovered a common theme in regard to friends. "Where are they?" is the question I hear the most. Patients talk about the absence of life long friends who are deeply missed. Where are they? Generally at home and afraid, because they don't know what to do with you. When you are dying it scares some people. I suspect you know that already before reading these words. In particular, it scares your friends because they may feel a responsibility to say something to you to make things better. And in the same breath, they realize they can say nothing. Equally, since many of your friends are of the approximate same age, your disease becomes a reminder that what is happening to you could just as easily be happening to them. And it will.

Well intentioned friends want to come and visit; they want to telephone and talk with you. Unfortunately, many of them are too frightened to do so. And after a certain period of time passes, the awkwardness turns to guilt. "What can I say to him?" one friend of a patient asked me, "I don't know any words. And besides that, over six months have passed since I last talked with him, and I can't find any explanation to give him that would be satisfying. How do I tell him that I am too uncomfortable to come and visit?"

If there are friends you wish to see before you die, and you haven't heard from them, maybe you can

If I Should Wake Before I Die

make it easier by calling and asking them to come around and see you. If you can't work up the energy to make the call, ask someone in your family to call them for you. Don't worry about "taking care" of your friends, or trying to make them feel better about your dying. If they have to struggle with this, so be it. In another way, this could be a tremendous gift to them, for sometime in their future, they will be walking the same path that you are now travelling.

If it is impossible for you to see some of your friends, don't hesitate to telephone and tell them how much their friendship has meant to you. Express those thoughts that you might have held back much of your life. And if you find you cannot do this, bring your friends into your mind and have a good "imaginary" conversation about old times and how greatly you enjoyed their presence in your life.

When you share truths with old friends, either in the quietness of your room, or over the telephone, or even in your mind, a great mystery unfolds. Rumi, the great Persian poet, writes that when two friends come together, "Christ becomes visible." Ever the storyteller, Rumi tells a magnificent story about two friends, a Mouse and a Frog, who would sit together by the river's edge in great conversation about deep spiritual matters. The Mouse, however, felt the absence of his good friend when the Frog was underwater, so a plan was devised in which a string was tied to the leg of the Mouse, with the other end attached to the Frog. In this way, they reasoned, they could be connected with each other at all times, and it would be a simple matter to contact one another by tugging on the string. Rumi calls this string a "long string, a longing string, so that by pulling on it their secret connection might be remembered."

Rumi continues the story with an unusual twist. A raven spots the Mouse on the river bank and swooping down, grabs him in his beak. As the raven soars upwards the Frog is tugged out of the water on the string attached to the Mouse. Rumi writes, "Amazed faces ask, 'When did a raven ever go underwater and catch a Frog?'"

The Frog answers, "This is the force of friendship. What draws friends together does not comform to the laws of nature." *(Mathnawi, VI, 2922-2973)*

And so it is with you and your friends. Whatever drew the two of you together with your wealth of experiences and stories, does not comform to the laws of nature. Give thanks, not only to God, for the joy of your many friends throughout your life, but also thank those friends, who are available, for the privilege of having them in your life. And for those friends who are not present, utter a silent prayer of gratitude and blessing for their souls having touched yours.

SHARED PAIN

The highest privilege there is,
is the privilege of being allowed
to share another's pain.
You talk about your pleasures
to your acquaintances;
You talk about your troubles
to your friends.

Fr. Andrew SDC,
Seven Words from the Cross.

If I Should Wake Before I Die

I CALL YOU FRIENDS

My commandment is this:
love one another just as I love you.
The greatest love a person can have
for his friends is to give his life for them.
And you are my friends if you do what I ask…
I do not call you servants
because a servant does not know
what his master is doing.
Instead I call you friends
because I have told you everything
I heard from my Father."

John 15:12-15

TRULY ONE

"Why should we two ever want to part?
Just as the leaf of the water-rhubarb
lives floating on the water,
we live as the great one and little one.
As the owl opens his eyes all night to the moon,
we live as the great one and little one.
This love between us
goes back to the first humans;
it cannot be annihilated.
Here is Kabir's idea:
As the river gives itself into the ocean
what is inside me moves inside you."

Kabir

Friendship

MORE MOUSE AND FROG

The mouse continues to say,
"My Friends, I know I'm ugly to you.
I'm ugly to me! I'm perfectly ugly!
But look, you'll be sad when I die, won't you?
You'll sit by my grave and weep a little?
All I'm asking is, be with me
that little bit of time while I'm still alive.
Now, I want you NOW!"

Rumi

PRAYING FOR YOUR FRIENDS

As long as Job stood against his friends
and his friends against him,
the attribute of divine justice prevailed;
Only after they made peace with each other,
And Job prayed for his friends,
The Holy One, blessed be He,
returned to him, as it is said:
"And the Lord turned the fortune of Job,
when he prayed for his friends."

Talmudic Sages

DOUBLING JOY

This communicating of man's self
to his friend works two contrary effects:
for it redoubleth joys,
and cutteth griefs in half.

Francis Bacon

God

God shall preserve
thy going out,
and thy coming in,
from this time forth
for evermore.

Psalm 121:8

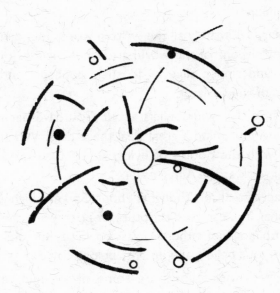

If I Should Wake Before I Die

What can be said about God that is not an opinion?

Nothing. Ultimately all the written words found in all the religions of the world are simply echoes of saints and sinner alike as to their concepts and beliefs of the Creator.

I am sure that your beliefs about God have been crossing your mind a great deal these days. When faced with the notion of dying, we all turn for a harder look at the Almighty.

The fact is that any thoughts about God are highly personal. You can read scripture or poetry and the wise opinions of others regarding God, but ultimately your beliefs and insights belong to you.

Therefore what follows are some of the nudges that have been helpful to me in my relationship with the Great Spirit of my life:

"God is like a parent who hides from a small child and then clears His throat to give Himself away."

Meister Eckhart

"God is the good, and all things which proceed from him are good."

Hildegarde of Bingen

"We are in God, and God, whom we do not see, is in us."

Julian of Norwich

"What sort of a God would it be, who only pushed from without?"

Goethe

"It is in God that we live, and move, and have our being."

Paul (Acts 17:28)

God

It is my sense that God is the holy and loving Force that lives within me. Equally, He is the Universal Spirit within which I live. And in that Divine Wind we all exist, either in the form of our bodies or in the figure of the angels.

Without God there is no "being." And with Him there is only Light and Love.

Some may wonder if I can justify any of these words I write about God. Of course, the answer is that God is never justified nor proven. He is only experienced at the Deepest Core of my existence. To say that God lives in my heart is no small exaggeration. In fact, to say that He flows in my breath is closer to the truth.

So much so that when I cease to inhale, He will carry me in His Breath.

There are those who wonder about the requirements of God. And while there are certain teachings which point to creeds and dogmas, I simply say that God loves you and will never let you go. The unconditional love of the Heavenly Parent does not keep score on the behavior of His children.

Instead, He embraces.

Let those who feel healthy enter theological debates. Perhaps when they find themselves short of breath and low on energy, the face of God will become more joyful.

For this day, allow the Love of God to fill you to overflowing and His peace to carry you through your fears.

LOOKING FOR GOD

The man who finds no taste of God wearies of looking for him. When one is looking for a thing and finds no trace of its existence

If I Should Wake Before I Die

one hunts half-heartedly and in distress.
But, lighting on some vestige of the quarry,
the chase grows lively, blithe and keen. The
man in quest of fire, cheered when he feels the
heat, looks for its source with eagerness and
pleasure. And so it is with those in quest of God:
feeling none of the sweetness of God they grow
listless but, sensing the sweetness of divinity,
they blithely pursue their search for God.

When a person goes out of himself
to find God, or fetch God, he is wrong.
I do not find God outside myself
nor conceive him excepting as my own
and in me.

Man's best chance of finding God
is where he left him.

Meister Eckhart

IN THE HEART

The Prophet said that God said,
"I am not contained in the container
of high and low, I am not contained
in the earth or all the heavens,
But I am contained
in the heart of My faithful servant.
How wonderful! If you seek Me, seek me there!"

Rumi

SEARCHING FOR GOD

Someone says, "I can't help feeding my family,
I have to work hard to earn a living."
He can do without God, but not without food;
he can do without Religion, but not without idols.
Where is the one who will say, "If I eat bread
without awareness of God, I will choke."

Rumi

God

THE PEACE OF GOD

The peace of God is shining in you now,
and from your heart extends around the world.
It pauses to caress each living thing,
and leaves a blessing with it that
remains forever and forever.
What it gives must be eternal.
It removes all thoughts of the valueless.
It brings renewal to all tired hearts,
and lights all vision as it passes by.
All of its gifts are given everyone, and everyone
unites in giving thanks to you who give,
and you who have received.

A Course in Miracles, Lesson 188

KNOWING THE ETERNAL

Eyes look but cannot see it,
Ears listen but cannot hear it,
Hands grasp but cannot touch it,
Beyond the senses lies the great Unity
     Invisible! Inaudible! Intangible!
What rises up appears bright,
What settles down appears dark,
Yet there is neither darkness nor light
just an unbroken dance of shadows.
From nothingness to fullness
and back again to nothingness.
The imageless Image cannot be grasped
by mind or might!

Try to face it,
     In what place will you stand?
Try to follow it,
     To what place will you go?

If I Should Wake Before I Die

Know That which is beyond all beginnings,
And you will know everything right here and now.
Know everything in this moment,
And you will know the Eternal.

Tao Te Ching

THE THIRSTY FISH

I laugh when I hear
that the fish in the water is thirsty.

You don't grasp the fact that what is most
alive of all is inside your own house;
and so you walk from one holy city,
to the next with a confused look.

Kabir will tell you the truth;
go wherever you like, to Calcutta or Tibet.
If you can't find where your soul is hidden,
for you the world will never be real!"

Kabir

PSALM 23

The Lord is my shepherd; I shall not want.
He makes me to lie down in green pastures,
He leads me beside still waters,
He restores my soul; He leads me in the path
of righteousness for His name's sake.
Yea, though I walk through the valley
of the shadow of death, I will fear no evil
For God is with me.
His rod and staff, they comfort me.

He prepares a table before me
in the presence of my enemies.
He anoints my head with oil; my cup runs over.
Surely goodness and mercy shall follow me
all the days of my life, and I will dwell
in the house of the Lord forever.

Guilt

How unhappy is he

who cannot forgive himself.

Publilius Syrus
Moral Sayings
1st century B.C.

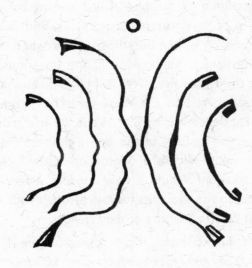

If I Should Wake Before I Die

The dying process is a time of enormous reflection, at least for most people. It is a looking back at a lifetime of joys, sorrows, successes, and failures. You tend to remember those times when major decisions were made with all the questions that those thoughts raise. "What if I had taken that job and transferred to the West Coast? What would have happened to my life? What if I had married this person instead of the one I chose? What if I had picked a different doctor, or refused chemo and radiation? Would it have made a difference?" And so on the thoughts ramble through your mind as you relive a lifetime of experiences.

In listening to hundreds of dying people, I have heard many expressed regrets over actions of the past, sometimes as long ago as half a century. A delightful poem by Edna St. Vincent Millay, written in 1939, says:

I have loved badly,
loved the great too soon,
withdrawn my words too late;
And eaten in an echoing hall
Alone and from a chipped plate
The words that I withdrew too late.

How many things in your past do you regret or wish you could live over again? At first blush, I imagine that many of you can think of several past accounts you would like to rearrange. And yet, there is an almost arrogant assumption in those thoughts, namely, that in looking back, you now know what would have been best for you. In reality, you probably don't have any idea whether a different decision "back then" would have made your life work any better or not.

Much more difficult than regret, it seems to me, are the feelings of guilt that you may suffer as you

Guilt

reflect back over your life. Guilt is such an incredible enemy of your inner peace. If you want to talk about disturbing the peace of God within, bring a guilty thought to consciousness. Guilt can visit you in the wee dark hours of the night and do a destructive dance in your head, keeping you awake until the early morning sun finds its way in your room.

As a therapist and chaplain, I can think of no greater demon to team with that old dragon, "fear," to destroy your sense of joy and comfort. Guilt and fear always are found together, sort of traveling companions so to speak. There's a good reason for this since one cannot exist without the other. Eric Hoffer, in "The Passionate State of the Mind," wrote "They who feel guilty are afraid, and they who are afraid somehow feel guilty." There is, however, a missing ingredient in all of this, namely, the force that Guilt always pushes towards — your punishment.

The Course in Miracles says that "Guilt asks for, and always receives punishment." In this true statement is the explanation of fear for the guilt-ridden person. If you are guilty of some terrible action in your past, or even think you are, then punishment must surely be coming just as the morning sun follows the night. Sitting squarely between guilt and punishment is fear. "You sit right there, young man," said my mother pointing to the sofa, "and you will get it when your father gets home." In this somewhat familiar family scene is the drama of guilt at work. "You did something wrong, you will be punished, and while you wait for the punishment to be inflicted, you will sit in fear."

How many of you are wondering about punishment for mistakes you have made in your life? And how does this struggle of the mind impact your anxiety, which in turn can affect the power of your

If I Should Wake Before I Die

pain medication? And for those of you who don't believe in puishment after death, do you seek a way to punish yourself while you're still alive? Or, perhaps you can suffer to atone for your guilt, and at the same time build up some "points," if there is an afterlife judgment and a scorekeeper.

My concern in all of this is the condemning self-judgments which drive the harshness of guilt home in your life. I have yet to meet a person who has called his "interior court" into session and **NOT** found himself/herself guilty! Perhaps now, today, is the time to see if there is another way to look at this. Regardless of how sick you may be, or how close to death, there is a way to let go of this horrid, demonic guilt in the embrace of Love and Peace.

The experts tell us there are two kinds of guilt: authentic and imaginary. In a sense this says there are things you have good reason to feel guilty over,

and other "sins" which are "in your head." My suggestion for you is that you begin to see that **ALL** guilt is imaginary. Oh, it is true that you can look at your life and see some "mistakes" you have made, but even those assume you know what was best for your life and soul. And my sense is that most of us in life haven't any idea about what was best.

Probably the biggest question is: do you want to let go of your judgments and the guilty conclusions you have reached as a part of your reflection process? If not, then, hold on tight and expect some difficult bumps along the way. Remember that guilt wants you to suffer. The question is: is that what you want?

If you want to let go, then there is only one step: to forgive yourself for the harsh judgments you have made. This means that you must be willing to "see your past differently," to look at your life

Guilt

through the window of self-love and grace, instead of the dark glass of self-condemning judgment. Your task is **NOT** to try to overlook your past mistakes, but to see that, even in those actions, the wisdom and guidance of God was moving. It isn't that those events didn't happen, they did. But the key to self-forgiveness is to understand it is your judgment of those "mistakes" that is the very thing that needs forgiving.

This is not an issue between you and God; instead it is an issue between you and you. The loving arms of God are already holding you. The question is: can you allow yourself the joy and peace that comes from such incredible Divine cradling? Only you are holding yourself back from those delights.

Some of you may be asking: doesn't God hold me accountable for my sins? My answer is that the "pardon" has already happened. You don't need to be crucified or punished when the prison doors have been flung open for your entire life; perhaps you just didn't know it.

Simply put, guilt is the most destructive force in the universe. You don't need it, especially now. It never helped you when you were healthy, and it certainly can't do anything positive for you now that you're dying. It will feed your fears and water your unhealthy need for punishment. But it doesn't have to be this way. Ask the spirit of God to help you let go of your needs for any punishment at all, and to open you heart to look at your life differently. Pray for guidance to see through the eyes of love and move toward healing, which, as Stephen Levine says, is "touching with loving-kindness and mercy those things you have heretofore touched with condemnation and self-hatred."

What a great gift to give to yourself as you prepare

to die. Truly, forgiveness of the self is a feeling within unlike any you have ever known. Grab it today!

NO INJURY

Guilty persons, even though the king had sentenced them to death, he did not cause to be killed, nor even looked on them with anger; he bound them with gentle words and with reform produced in their character — even their release was accompanied by no inflicted injury.

Buddah-Karita, Bk. II.42

THE SOURCE OF SORROW

Guilt is the source of sorrow, the avenging fiend, that follows behind with whips and stings.

Rowe

GUILT OR GUILTLESSNESS?

*Each day, each hour and minute,
even each second, you are deciding
between the crucifixion and the resurrection;
between the ego and the Holy Spirit.
The ego is the choice of guilt;
the Holy Spirit is the choice for guiltlessness.
The power of decision is all that is yours.
What you can decide between is fixed,
because there are no alternatives except truth
and illusion. And there is no overlap between
them because they are opposites, which
cannot be reconciled and cannot both be true.
You are guilty or guiltless,
bound or free, unhappy or happy.*

Course In Miracles, Ch. 14, P. 255

GOD LOVES US

Love says, "I will deliver you this instant!"
I groped for excuses, but love came excusing me.
I don't feel strange anymore
with my heart here, my soul there.
I discovered He is heart and soul.

It was He, not I, knocking at the door
It was He within.
I caress my own breast for there He is hidden.

No one else knows you,
Since you are I, I know you.
Forms become a trifle when
feeling and intuition richly intensify.
In the end a man tires of everything
except heart's desiring, soul's journeying.

Sultan, saint, pickpocket;
love has everyone by the ear,
dragging us to God by secret ways.
I never knew that God, too, desires us.

Rumi, translation by Daniel Liebert

THE CHOICE IS YOURS

I give you now the choice between life and death,
between blessing and curse,
and I call heaven and earth
to witness the choice you make.
Choose Life!

Deuteronomy 30:19

If I Should Wake Before I Die

NOTHING TO DO WITH SIN

As Jesus was walking along,
he saw a man who had been born blind.
His disciples asked him, "Teacher,
whose sin caused him to be born blind?
Was it his own or his parents' sin?"

Jesus answered, "His blindness has nothing
to do with his sins or his parents sins.
He is blind so that God's power
might be seen at work in him…"

After he said this, Jesus spat on the ground
and made some mud with the spittle;
he rubbed the mud on the man's eyes
and told him, "Go and wash your face
in the Pool of Siloam." So the man went,
washed his face, and came back seeing.

John 9:1-3, 6-7

Healing

The whole point of this life
is the healing of the heart's eye
through which God is seen.

St. Augustine of Hippo

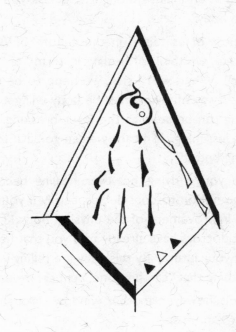

If I Should Wake Before I Die

Healing is an infinite thought... unless you limit it to the body.

For most of us raised in the culture of Western medicine, we think of healing in terms of "getting better." When we're sick, we hope to be healed, another way of saying that the body will get better. Healing can be seen as the fever breaking, or the cough lessening. It means we can go back to work "feeling better."

When you're dying, however, healing becomes a strange notion to consider, especially if your focus is the improvement of the physical body. The fact is that doctors have already told you that healing is not in your future. By this, they are telling you that everything that "can be done has been done."

There is, however, another window through which healing can be seen.

Looking at life as an experience which is beyond the physical is a necessity if you expect to discover any sort of healing for yourself at this time. And since you have accepted the fact that your body is not going to heal, it becomes vitally important to your sense of well being to understand the concept of "inner healing."

Healing means to "make whole," which is another way of saying that the wounded and hurting parts of you — those parts which have been splintered — need to be put back together. Inner healing is when you allow God to touch those injured parts that have caused you so much pain throughout your life, and in that touch to transform the hurts into joys.

"Inner healing is simply this," writes Francis MacNutt, "God can take the memories of our past and heal them… and fill with His love all those places in us that have been empty for so long." As difficult as it is to believe, our souls ache for the peace and joy which comes from the light and love of God. What seems to get in the way of our experience of joy is the pain and resentment of the past.

Inner healing is a letting go of those injuries and judgments which have been kept within for so long. As John Townroe writes, "It releases the person from the emotional grip of the past."

It seems to me, in my experience as a therapist, that the pain and struggles of the past does an incredible number on our health and well-being. There are hundreds of clients with whom I have spent hours in conversation — physically healthy people, I might add — whose inner being is so devastated by the wounds of the past that they are living lives which border on paralysis.

If healing had to do with the body, these people would be extremely healthy folks. Instead, they are the walking wounded, making their way through life in pain and suffering. When the doctor pronounces them terminal with Stage V Cancer, their need for healing remains as powerful as it did prior to their illness.

Physical sickness has little to do with the need for healing. Terminal illness only serves to point you to the urgency of embracing the healing Force within. A sick spirit, rooted in past injuries, cries out for the healing salve which leads to wholeness.

Inner healing is a matter of forgiveness, love, and the release of all judgments. Not only will you feel better physically, by the way, but your spirit will begin singing, a sound you have not heard in a long, long time.

If I Should Wake Before I Die

At this time in your life, outer healing will probably not occur. Inner healing, however, is a real and transforming possibility. While your mind is clear and your spirit willing, why not reach within to change your judgments into loving thoughts and your anger into forgiveness.

LIFE GIVING WATER

Jesus said, "Whoever drinks this water will get thirsty again, but whoever drinks the Water that I will give him will never be thirsty again.

The water that I will give him will become in him a living spring which will provide him with life-giving water and give him eternal life."

John 4:13, 14

BECOMING SATISFIED

The Lord says,
"Come everyone who is thirsty —
here is Water!
Come you who have not money,
buy grain and eat!
Why spend money on what does not satisfy?
Why spend your wages and still be hungry?
Listen to me and hear what I say,
And you will enjoy the best food of all."

Isaiah 55:1-3

TRUE HEALTH

For true health, we have to forgive God, others, and ourselves.

Phillip Pare

Healing

THE SPIRIT WITHIN

However broken down
is the spirit's shrine,
the spirit is there all the same.

Nigerian Proverb

RELEASING THE PAST

Every situation properly perceived
becomes an opportunity to heal.

Could you but recognize for a single instant
the power of healing that the reflection of God
shining in you, can bring to all the world,
you could not wait to make the mirror of your
mind clean to receive the image of the
holiness that heals the world.

A Course in Miracles, Text P. 271

SURRENDER

"There's a necessary dying for all of us,
then Jesus is breathing again.

Very little grows on jagged rock.
Be ground.

Be crumpled so wildflowers will come up
where you are.

You've been stony for too many years.
Try something different.
Surrender."

Rumi:
A Necessary Autumn
Inside Each Of Us.

If I Should Wake Before I Die

Hope

Even now I am full of hope,
but the end lies in God.

Pindar

If I Should Wake Before I Die

Hope is a tough act in the midst of dying.

In all probability, you wouldn't be reading this if somehow or other the medical community had not pronounced a terminal sentence on your body. Like all of us, you are dying. Life is, after all, a terminal condition. Unlike most of us, however, you have moved into the active stage.

Some people reading this will feel these words are morbid. You, however, are working on moving past such thinking. To be actively dying is to move beyond the world of pretense and game playing. Life is truly too short to tell lies anymore. Surrendering to the admission of dying is only one of several courageous moves you have already made in this unknown journey.

So, how does hope enter into this process called dying?

Hearing a doctor say that his cancer is no longer treatable and that he should go home and get his affairs in order, a patient screams from the waiting room, "What right do you have to take away my hope?"

The real question is: what is my hope when my condition is terminal? It certainly is possible to hope to die pain free. Or to not die at all, or at least to not die now. Except that we all know that even if we trick the grim reaper today, he will discover our hiding place tomorrow.

Seen for what it truly is, hope never rests in the expectation that you won't die.

It is, however, a pointing toward the future. But not in the miracle of a disappearing tumor, regardless of how wonderful that would be. There are those reading these words who will get better, for a

Hope

short time or a long time. But hope is not about getting better.

Instead, it is about transformation.

In *Letter to a Priest,* Simon Weil writes, "The virtue of hope is an orientation of the soul towards a transformation after which it will be wholly and exclusively love."

Hope, in order to be realistic, can never be separated from the real you. It points to the truth that you are more than blood and bones. Body thinking and hope are short-lived bed fellows. Hope points to the transformation of the real you from your current address to another.

When the caterpillar enters the cocoon, there would be a certain amount of silliness in its saying, "I hope I'll get better." Rather, the hope is in the transformation that occurs from a fuzzy, crawling, limited creature to the butterfly that soars in the sunshine.

The miracle is that both creatures are one in the same.

Hoping for a miracle is another way of anticipating a transformation from the limited existence of the body to the love-soaring life of your Soul.

Regardless of your theology, there is great hope in the possibility of transformation. Beginning today, you could tell your inquiring friends and family members when they ask you how you're doing, "I'm transforming!"

Smile when you say it.

If I Should Wake Before I Die

TRANSFORMING

The body is a limit.
Who would seek for freedom in a body
looks for it where it can't be found.

Who transcends the body
has transcended limitation.

A Course in Miracles,
T. Ch. 19, P. 372

A GRAIN OF FAITH

A man with a grain of faith in God
never loses hope,
because he ever believes
in the ultimate triumph of Truth.

Gandhi

BLESSINGS FROM GOD

"I will bless the person
who puts his hope in me.
He is like a tree growing near a stream
and sending out roots to the water.
It is not afraid when hot weather comes,
because its leaves stay green;
It has no worries when there is no rain,
it keeps on bearing fruit."

Jeremiah 17:7, 8

LOOKING AHEAD

Forgetting those things which are behind
and reaching forth unto those things which
are before, I press toward the mark.

Philippians 3:13, 14

HOPE FOR THE SPIRIT

For it was by hope that we were saved,
but if we see what we hope for,
then it is not really hope.
For who hopes for something he sees?

But if we hope for what we do not see,
we wait for it in patience.
In the same way,
the Spirit also comes to help us,
weak as we are.
For we do not know
how we ought to pray,
the Spirit himself
pleads with God for us
in groans that words cannot express.

And God, who sees into our hearts,
knows what the thought of the Spirit is,
because the Spirit pleads with God
on behalf of his people
and in accordance with His will."

Romans 8:26, 27

HOPE FOR THE CREATOR

Phillip once said:
"Lord, show us the Father
and it is enough for us."
Do you want the marrow
out of which goodness springs?
Do you want the nucleus
from which goodness flows?
Do you want the root, the vein,
from which goodness exudes?
And all beauty?
Then you seek the Creator.
And you want your breakthrough.

For remember this:
The shell must be cracked open
if what is inside is to come out.
If you want the kernel
you must break the shell.
We must learn to break through things
if we are to grasp God in them.

Meister Eckhart

Laughter

Pain is deeper than all thought;
Laughter is higher than all pain.

Elbert Hubbart

If I Should Wake Before I Die

There are those, I suppose, who would have you think there is nothing funny at all about dying. And I'm sure they have a point. But overall, there's a lot to laugh about in both living and dying. A good chuckle can do you a world of good. Finding something to laugh at in the middle of a whole lot of crap, seems like a worthwhile endeavor to me. When my father was dying, he would struggle with confusion. Holding the portable telephone and pointing it towards the TV, he would furiously push the buttons attempting to change channels. As it dawned on him that he did not have the remote control, but was instead punching a telephone, he would break into a big grin. Then we would all laugh together. It also made us feel better for a short time.

Chamfort wrote that "the most wasted day of all is that in which we have not laughed." It was in 1805 that he wrote those words, but they ring especially true today. Dying is tough business. It carries with it more than its share of pain and sorrow. Each night you can struggle with difficult or fearful thoughts. There is the constant living in uncertainty with the possibility of daily losses. If you can find something to laugh at it in all of this, as the commercial says, why not grab all the gusto you can get? Perhaps a good joke can be as healing as one of those many pills you take. Or even a bad joke. A man went to a doctor who told him, "I've got bad news for you. You could go at any time." The man said, "Great! I haven't gone for five days." Now, I think that's funny. I also realize that there's nothing humorous about constipation. It's one of the things you live with if you take pain medication. So, if it's a given as a trade off for relief, why not laugh about it? My suspicion is that when we die, a whole lot

Laughter

of those things which we have taken seriously in this life will appear somewhat ridiculous. Emmanuel writes that one of the first things we do when we die is break out in laughter. I've often wondered how we would approach death if we truly remembered our true nature? Knowing that our worn out bodies will be put down while we soar into spirit might be enough to bring a smile to our faces. One of the most wonderful experiences of living in spiritual trust is the feeling of intense Joy. And a key symptom of that joy is laughter. So don't be afraid to look around and find things to laugh at in your current plight. Milton Berle writes "I've got bad arthritis but I can't kick."

That line won't cure his arthritis, but it will surround it with the light of laughter. Years ago, when diagnosed with cancer, Norman Cousins contributed enormously to his healing with laughter. He laughed through rented movies and silly jokes, dumping powerful healing chemicals into his blood stream.

Laughter heals. If not the body, then the spirit. What more could you want? Oh, another joke. Well, an old man was dying and he smelled the aroma of fresh-baked cookies. He said to his wife, "Can I have one of your cookies?" "Absolutely not," his wife answered, "You know they're for the wake." Smile and laugh and be joyful. It's great medicine for you.

If I Should Wake Before I Die

LAME AND LAUGHING

Then Hephaistos poured wine
to all the other gods from right to left,
ladling the sweet nectar from the bowl.
And laughter unquenchable arose amid
the blessed God to see Hephaistos bustling
through the palace.

The Iliad, Bk.I

WEEPING AND LAUGHING

Happy are you poor,
the Kingdom of God is yours!
Happy are you who are hungry now,
you will be filled!
Happy are you who weep now;
you will laugh!

Jesus

THE HEAVENS SHOOK

"Then this young Goddess, Uzume,
commenced to tread with measure
upon the circular hollow box and cause it
to resound; sang a six syllable song or
charm of numbers; and gradually quickening
her dance, such a spirit descended upon the
Goddess that she loosened her dress,
revealing more and more of her loveliness,
and at last, to the intense amusement
of the Gods, discarded her dress all together.
With the laughter of the Gods
the heavens shook!"

The Nihongi

Laughter

DYING, LAUGHING

A lover was telling his Beloved
how much he loved her,
how faithful he had been,
how self-sacrificing,
getting up at dawn every morning,
fasting, giving up wealth
and strength and fame for her.
There was a fire in him.
He didn't know where it came from,
but it made him weep
and melt like a candle.
"You've done well," she said,
"but listen to me:

"All this is the decor of love,
the branches and leaves and blossoms. You
must live at the root
to be a True Lover."
"Where is that? Tell me?"
"You've done the outward acts,
but you haven't died. You must die."
When he heard that, he lay back on the
ground, laughing and died.
He opened like a rose that drops
to the ground and died laughing.
That laughter was his freedom
and his gift to the Eternal.

Rumi,
Translated by Coleman Barks

BEING HAPPY

To be whole-hearted,
you must be happy.
If fear and love cannot co-exist,
and if it is impossible
to be wholly fearful
and remain alive,
the only possible whole state
is that of love.
There is no difference
between love and joy.
Therefore, the only possible
whole state is that of love."

Course In Miracles, Ch. 5, P. 66

LOSS

I do not fear death

as much as I fear dependence.

The Living Will

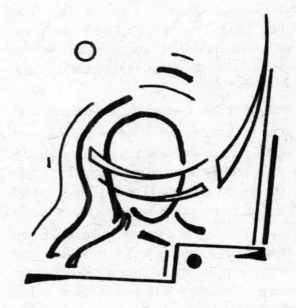

If I Should Wake Before I Die

Some say that loss begins when you leave your mother's womb and continues on a daily basis until you die. "Loss is nothing else but change, and change is Nature's delight," wrote Marcus Aurelius. However, I do not think that he meant loss is some kind of a treat in life.

For most of us, loss is terrifying and difficult.

It may be the basis on which we build our powerful defense mechanisms which take us through life with some meager attempt at protection. If I am hurt enough through life's changes, I will do the best I can to shield myself against further pain.

Loss is a reminder of our own vulnerability and defenselessness. From the first time we lose a pet or grandparent, we are on guard. Searching for safety in a world where it cannot be found, we still struggle to keep loss at a distance.

Rarely does our strategy work.

The fear of loss and the attempt at control walk hand in hand. Trying to keep loss or change away necessitates the need for more controls in life. It can be exhausting at best, and depressing at worse.

If you're reading this, you have already learned the hard lesson that there are some things you just can't control. Sickness leads to several experiences of loss. You can no longer count on your body to do what you want it to do. Muscles that once were strong now quiver with weakness when you simply try to hold a book. The loss of body strength is a given in the dying process.

Not only are you struggling with the multi-losses of your illness, you are anticipating the loss of everything and everyone you know. Regardless of your faith in transformation and the other side, it is

Loss

impossible to ignore the pain and sorrow of expected losses in this life.

To my knowledge, there is only one place to hold on when loss is crashing all around you. It is to the absolute unshakable Spirit of God, which transcends this side and the other as the Changeless. Spread-eagling two worlds, God carries you through the daily losses from here to there.

Without the Unchangeable, there is no place to cling. God is the force which stands when all else has fallen away, and by now you know how much of your life can be truly shaken.

Some time ago, I bought a book which was not very interesting. There was, however, a bookmark inside with a quotation which said: "Attachment is the greatest form of self-cruelty." I thought about that for a long time, eventually seeing the wisdom in the words.

Attaching to the changeable is, indeed, a cruel notion, for it means that you are holding on to that which may slip at any moment. That includes your body's strength or the functions of your organs.

Attaching to the Unchangeable Presence is the only action that makes sense in a world where we are terminal at birth. There is no way out of this life without loss. Holding on to God carries us through the chaos; anything else is only a temporary fix.

Embrace the Spirit now and draw peace for yourself from the losses which keep rolling in like fog from the sea. God is the only Anchor which holds, and His spirit is the safety for the rest of your boat ride.

If I Should Wake Before I Die

A CRAZY IDEA

To refuse the sweets of life
because they once must leave us,
is as preposterous as to wish
to have been born old
because we one day must be old.

William Congreve
The Way of the World, 1700

RESURRECTION

"For since by man came death,
by man came also the resurrection of the dead.
For as in Adam (the personality), all die,
so all in Christ (Spirit)
shall all be made alive."

I Corinthians 15:21, 22

LOSING YOUR RAFT

A man walking along a highroad
sees a great river, its near bank
dangerous and frightening,
its far bank safe.
He collects sticks and foliage,
makes a raft, paddles across the river
and reaches the other shore.
Now suppose that,
after he reaches the other shore,
he takes the raft and puts it on his head
and walks with it on his head
wherever he goes.
Would he be using the raft
in an appropriate way?

Loss

No, a reasonable man will realize
that the raft has been very useful
to him in crossing the river
and arriving safely on the other shore,
but that once he has arrived,
it is proper to leave the raft behind
and walk on without it..
This is using the raft appropriately.
In the same way, all truths should be used
to cross over; they should not be
held on to once you have arrived.
You should let go of even the most profound
insight or the most wholesome teaching,
all the more so, unwholesome teachings.

The Buddha

ALL WE HAVE IS NOW

What is born will die,
What has been gathered will be dispersed,
What has been accumulated will be exhausted,
What has been built up will collapse,
And what has been high will be brought low.

The Buddha

NO LOSSES

Let us not be afraid to love our dear ones,
foolishly fearing to lose them in the mists
of death. Love them so dearly, so truly,
so purely and forever unlamentingly —
even in temporary, love-kindling separation
that you find in them the everlasting,
true love of God.

Paramahansa Yogananda

109

If I Should Wake Before I Die

DEDICATION TO LIFE

What is death to you?
Your dedication is not to death,
nor to its master.
When you accepted
the Holy Spirit's purpose
in place of the ego's,
you renounced death,
exchanging it for life.
We know that an idea
leaves not its source.
And death is the result of the thought
we call the ego, as surely as life
is the result of the Thought of God.

A Course in Miracles, Text, P. 388

Love

Love is all we have,
the only way that each
can help the other.

Euripides

If I Should Wake Before I Die

When you are dying, talk of love gets messy and confusing. For many of us, the thought of leaving those persons who mean the most to us in the whole world, is equated with the loss of all love. You can lie in your bed and watch your husband or wife, son or daughter, bring you a glass of water or fluff up your pillow, and in that moment feel so filled with love that you can barely stand to see them leave the room. The preciousness of life and relationship seems to shatter every moment when you consider the fact that you will not be in your body for much longer.

It seems as though there is an awareness throughout life that the more you allow yourself to love, the greater your vulnerability to the potential losses that most surely will occur. Loving others places you at risk, and nowhere can it be more powerfully felt than in your mind and heart when you are dying. How often have I stood in the room of a patient, with the family surrounding the bed, and felt the love filling the room to the point where I felt my heart would burst. At those moments, love and pain seem to go hand in hand.

But without the expression and feeling of love, where would life take you except to loneliness and separation? It is true that you might be safe in your hermit cave of self-protection, but you would find life rushing by without your participation. Back in 1699 Francois Fenelon wrote that "to love nothing is not to live without love, but feebly is to languish rather than live." Simply put, without love, life is sterile movement through a colorless room.

The fact is that most of us know love as the core part of our being, but the creation of our defense system in response to childhood wounding can often diminish that knowledge. You may know the

Love

beauty and joy of loving others in your lifetime, but the cost of that love may be seen as too expensive, given your history of being hurt in relationships. And yet, what else is there to do if you are to be a true participant in the playing field called the world? Your soul cries out for you to leave the sidelines and become who you truly are.

The enemy of love is fear, and how tremendously powerful is that dragon! You may avoid love because of the fear of being hurt or rejected, or you may be fearful of your own motives, or second guess your actions. Sometimes there is the fear that something is wrong with you, and that others would not want your love anyway, or worse, would not meet your love with their own. Fear is that part of you that suggests it is safer to be alone than to risk loving another.

Probably the greatest fear of loving is the potential loss of the self. I remember when I was a child listening to missionaries speak in our church. They would show slides of deplorable conditions in third world countries, all for the purpose of encourging church members to financially support their work. At the conclusion of their presentation, the minister would ask a most dreaded question: "Is God calling anyone here this evening to be a missionary?"

I remember sitting with my eyes closed, begging God not to call me to become one of His missionaries. Being sent to some God-awful land where potato chips and color televisions were absent, seemed to be more than I could bear. My fear was, of course, that if God (love) spoke to me, I would have to respond. There would be no choice. And in that call I visioned the loss of my self. It seemed as though if I gave myself to God's love, there would no longer be a me.

If I Should Wake Before I Die

Because many of us fear a similar loss of self, we hold back from total love, only to discover that loss will appear regardless. Eric Fromm wrote in 1955, "Love is union with somebody, or something, outside oneself, under the condition of retaining the separateness and integrity of one's own self." My suspicion is that this is meant to be a positive statement, but in reality, Fromm has stated the struggle that most of creation shares, namely, how to love without getting lost.

As you read these words, you may be reflecting on the times in your life that you have loved only partially. Most of us can make such a statement. But you see, the problem with such a reflection is that it is a self-condemning judgment of past behavior, without taking into account the level of your fear. We all could examine dozens of experiences in our histories where we didn't love enough, or were too protective of ourselves. This is the nature of being human.

What gets lost in this unkind judgment is the profound and deep awareness that regardless of your lack of loving behavior, you ARE love. No matter how many times, nor how many ways you have failed to be loving toward others, you still are the creation and extension of Love itself. This makes you part of the Creative Source of all of life, a being of Love. Whether you practice it or not is immaterial to who you are!

This truly is a most important thought: you are Love, breathing and alive in a body. It is true that fear and pain may have kept you from expressing this love in its fullest form, but nevertheless, you came from Love and to Love you will return. As a matter of fact, everyone who cares for you or who enters your room came from Love also. We all are

Love

extensions of the Loving power which created the world, and therefore, at our deepest level, are Loving one another all the time. Is it possible for you to imagine your soul joining in a loving way with the souls of your family members and friends? Perhaps they are playing together, delighting in the absolute knowledge that you, and everyone, is safe in the Loving arms of the Source of all creation.

Don't worry so much about love being an action verb. Instead, rejoice in the Loving being that you **ARE.** And express your gratitude to the God of all Love for making you a part of His plan for the world. As Ladislaus Boros wrote in the *Time of Temptation,* "God created the world out of pure love, since He can do nothing other than love…" Or as the Course in Miracles says, "Love will enter immediately into any mind that truly wants it, but it must want it truly. Your task is not to seek for love but merely to seek and find all of the barriers within yourself that you have built against it. See the love of God in you, and you will see it everywhere because it is everywhere. Love, which created me, is what I am."

GROWING LOVE

Only Love is true, vital, wise.
As Love grows in you,
God grows in you.
In your Love you become
organic with God.
When you are naught but Love,
you are the express image
of His person.

E. W. Lewis

THE LOVE FLOW

Effortlessly, Love flows from God into man,
Like a bird who rivers the air
Without moving her wings.
Thus we move in His world
One in body and soul,
Though outwardly separate in form,
As the Source strikes the note,
Humanity sings — The Holy Spirit
is our Harpist, and all strings
Which are touched in Love Must sound.

Mechthild of Magdeburg
Translated by Jane Hirshfield

IN HIS IMAGE

To say that I am made in the Image of God
is to say that Love is the reason for my existence,
for God is love.
Love is my true identity…
Love is my true character…
Love is my name.

Thomas Merton

WE LOVE BECAUSE...

We love because He first loved us.

I John 4:19

LOVE

Love wakes much and sleeps little,
even in sleeping does not sleep.
It faints yet is not weary; it is restricted
in its liberty yet is in great freedom.
It sees reason to fear, but does not fear,
but, like an ember or a spark of fire,
flames always upward, by the fervor
of its love, toward God, and through
the special help of grace
is delivered from all perils and dangers.
He who is thus a spiritual lover
knows well what that voice means which says:
You, Lord God, are my whole love and desire.
You are all mine, and I all Yours.

Dissolve my heart into Your love so that
I may know how sweet it is to serve You

and how joyful it is to praise You,
and to be as though I were all melded
into Your love.

Thomas a Kempis

If I Should Wake Before I Die

LOVE IS...

I may be able to speak the languages of men
and even of angels, but if I have no love,
my speech is no more than a noisy gong
or a clanging bell.
I may have the gift of inspired preaching;
I may have all knowledge and understand
all secrets; I may have all the faith needed
to move mountains — but if I have no love,
I am nothing.
I may give away everything I have,
and even give up my body to be burned —
but if I have not love, this does me no good.

Love is patient and kind;
it is not jealous or conceited or proud;
love is not ill-mannered or selfish or irritable;
love does not keep a record of wrongs,
love is not happy with evil
but is happy with the truth.
Love never gives up; and its faith, hope,
and patience never fail.
Love is eternal.

I Corinthians 13:1-8

118

Medication

*Most men die
of their remedies,
not of their diseases.*

Moliere (1673)

If I Should Wake Before I Die

If you're like most dying people, your nightstand is littered with bottles of pills. There are those little brown containers with the caps that you can't remove and names you can't pronounce. If you're lucky, maybe you have some of those liquid medicines that come with their own plastic cup so you don't have to dirty a spoon.

All medicines end up costing you something beyond money.

You can take a narcotic for pain control, and it might work fairly well, although you will probably be confused and out of it for a couple of days while your body adjusts to the medicine. Of course, it will make you constipated, so you'll need to send someone out to pick up a bottle of laxatives or stool softeners.

With all medications, there are trade-offs.

But even with all of these complaints, there is enormous gratitude for the relief and healing qualities of medicine. It can help you sleep and allow you enough comfort to enjoy a conversation with a friend. Medicine sometimes carries us over the hard places when we cannot get there by ourselves.

There is a chance, however, that you may be overlooking one of the most powerful medicines available to you, and that is the healing, soothing power that sits within your own mind. Shakespeare recognized this when he wrote, "Our remedies oft in ourselves do lie, Which we ascribe to heaven."

Consider the possibility that living within you is the guiding force of much healing that we call nature. Back in 1588 Montaigne wrote in an essay, "The general order of things that takes care of fleas and moles also takes care of men, if they will have the

Medication

same patience that fleas and moles have, to leave it to itself."

All of this is another way of saying that your mind carries enormous power for relief from pain. And this is not to state that you can "think" away your discomfort, but rather that you can develop an openness and trust which will allow the normal and natural flow of "internal" medicine to do its work.

In my business, we call this "Spiritual energy" at work. As you open yourself to trusting that power and love of God, you create channels for Spiritual movement within your body. In a sense, the more open and trusting you are, the more effective your medication becomes. It is a working together of the scientific wonder of your pills with the Spiritual opening of your body.

Medication is both external and internal. When you swallow a pill, it begins to work hand in hand with the cells of your body. Equally, as you allow Spiritual energy to flow through your being, those same cells are affected. Medication is not only something you hold in your hand, it is the power that rests with you in every breath.

Love is a grand medication, as is trust and hope. Being surrounded with those who care about you is great medicine. Learning how to forgive the injuries and wounds of the past releases pain more effectively than Morphine. Meditating on the wonder and care of God can place you in a wondrous place where you no longer feel the heaviness of pain.

Meditation as medication is a tool that we all need to learn. And you're never too old to learn, or too sick. Below is a meditation that you can use to help bring a sense of peace and comfort to you right now. If you're too tired or weak to read it, have someone read it to you. Or record it to listen to before you go to sleep.

When you're dying, why not try all means for physical, emotional and mental release? You'll probably be surprised... and delighted!

A MEDITATION

Make sure that you find a comfortable place to rest. Your bed, favorite chair, or sofa will work very well. And try to relax as peacefully as possible against the pillow or cushion. Before you begin, ask God to help you to rest in Him during the meditation.

Begin by breathing as deeply as you can. Allow your lungs to fill with as much air as you can comfortably take in... breathing in and out in a slow rhythmic manner. Just breathe in and out, following the in and out motion with your mind. Focus on your breathing and try to allow all other thoughts to float away from your mind. If an unpleasant thought crosses your mind, pretend it is a small cloud and gently push it aside.

With each breath you inhale, begin to imagine that you are breathing in the light and love of God... in and out with God's light and love. Simply allow all of the organs of your body to fill with God's light and love. Breathing in and out... in and out... in and out.

And as you breathe in God's love, begin to imagine that with each out-breath, you are filling all of the space around you with God's light and love. Soon all of your space will be filled with God's love. As you breathe in and out, you will discover that God's presence is filling your entire being as well as all of the space around you.

Medication

Rest comfortably with the thought that God is completely upholding you, both from within and without. And now as you breathe in and out, you will find yourself relaxing in His care. Just breathe in and out,… in and out… and allow the peace to flow over you.

If you have special fears or cares, you can take a moment now and imagine placing all of those worries in a beautiful white box. Put them in there one by one until you have placed all of your concerns inside. Then simply hand the box over to God, who will take in and handle each one of those fears and worries with love and comfort.

As you now rest in God's presence, allow your mind to peacefully help you drift to sleep, or simply relax in His care. Remember to breathe comfortably, in and out… in and out… and allow the healing of loving thoughts to care for you.

FROM THE TEMPLE STREAM

On each bank of the stream,
all kinds of trees will grow to provide food.
Their leaves will never wither,
and they will never stop bearing fruit.
They will have fresh fruit every month,
because they are watered by the same stream
that flows from the Temple.
The trees will provide food,
and their leaves will be used
as medicine for healing people.

Ezekiel 47:12

TO MAKE YOU SMILE

Injections are the best thing
ever invented for feeding doctors.

Gabriel Garcia Marquez

If I Should Wake Before I Die

GOD AND MEDICINE

God hath created medicines out of the earth,
And let not a discerning man reject them.
Was not the water made sweet by the wood,
That He might make known
to all men His power?
And He gave men discernment,
That they might glory in His mighty works.
By means of them,
the physician assuageth pain,

And likewise the apothecary
prepareth a confection:
That His work may not cease,
Nor health from the face of the earth.

From the Wisdom of Ben Sera
(Sirach)

SEARCHING

It is medicine and not scenery
for which most sick men go searching.

Seneca, *Letters to Lucilius*

THE HEALING PLANT

Whatever man shall flatter Homa (plant)
as a young son, Homa comes to the aid
of him and his children, to be their medicine.
Homa! Give me some of the healing powers
whereby thou art my physician."

Homa Yasht, Haug

Meditation

Who looks outside dreams —
Who looks inside wakes.

Carl Jung

If I Should Wake Before I Die

I remember my first, and only time, that I went to the stock car races. My older cousin, whom I worshipped and adored, was a racing fanatic, who decided in a rare moment of generosity to invite me to accompany him to the races one Friday night. I remember two things about that evening: the bright lights and the cars roaring past our bleacher seats with a deafening noise. After a while I was lost in the noise and speed of each car thundering past our seats.

Today that stock car race reminds me of my thoughts. They whiz in and out of my brain like those cars buzzing around that race track circle. Every time I find myself in a difficult situation, or facing something fearful, my thoughts race through my brain one after another. Sleeping becomes impossible, or if I do manage to fall asleep, when I wake up the thoughts are waiting at the starting gate to begin their speedy parade.

As I have talked with hundreds of dying people, I have found that the "racing mind syndrome" is one commonly shared by all. When fear is present the mind kicks into high gear, as the frightening thoughts quickly enter and leave, only to be replaced by new, and perhaps more fearful ones.

When I was a child and had bad dreams, I remember calling to my father that I was afraid. His advice was probably like that of many parents: "Think about something else," he would say. That was easy advice for him, but lying in the dark, with the possibility of ghosts and goblins leaping onto my bed, seemed almost impossible for me to do.

In the book of Psalms is written, "Be still and know that I am God." This passage, regardless of how comforting it may sound, is far from easy to do when you are actively dying. How can you be "still"

Meditation

when you have no idea what tomorrow will bring? How can you be "still" when you are uncertain if your pain medication will hold, or your bowels will move? Or how can you quiet your mind when the Doctor told you there are three months left to live, and two have already rushed by? What do you do when your mind will not rest and you are weary beyond the need for sleep?

It is one thing to suggest stilling the mind, and quite another to find the skills to make it happen. With all the talk these days about meditation and inner peace, what does it really mean and how can it help you in the fearful spaces of your mind? Max Kauffman, in a humorous line said, "My son has taken up meditation — at least it's better than sitting and doing nothing." But in reality, that is a large part of what meditation is all about. It is "doing nothing" except "being" in the presence of God, or whatever you choose to call that comforting Source within. And to be quite honest, most of us haven't the slightest idea what that means or how to even begin to approach meditation.

There's not much sense in writing a great deal about how difficult you may find just "being," since you have probably spent most of your life "doing." It's the way of the Western world to "do," and often there are financial or cultural rewards for how much you actually can "do." The plain fact is that we don't know how to just "be." And my guess is that you have been struggling with "being" as you have been allowing others in your life to take care of you.

In a simple sort of way, meditation is "being" with God. It is a time when you slow down your thoughts enough that there is space of God to enter with some peace and calmness. In my way of thinking, meditation is like that stock car race I mentioned in the beginning of this chapter. Your thoughts race by like those cars, speeding one after another, all day and night. Meditation is slowing the thoughts, just like those cars would slow down, until you are focused on the space between the cars. It is finding a way to interrupt the racing, fearful thoughts, so that you allow the comfort of God to enter in the silence between. Being still does not mean simply being quiet, although that is usually a necessary part of meditating, it also means "stilling" the speeding mind, calming the racing thoughts.

The native Americans have a saying: A busy mind is a sick mind; a slow mind is a healthy mind; and a still mind is a Divine mind. In meditation you allow for the merger of the holy inside you with the holy that surrounds you. It is only your thoughts that keep the peace-filled experience from happening.

God, and his peace, is not kept outside your mind and heart by skin and bones, instead He is kept at bay by the busyness and fearfulness of your thoughts.

Sometimes people ask if there is a difference between prayer and meditation. That's probably a question that cannot be answered, but in my view, prayer tends to be those times we talk to God about our concerns, needs, or desires. Meditation, on the other hand, is the time God fills us with His presence. Both prayer and meditation are about connecting with the Holy, but often prayer gets focused "out," while meditation is the time when the mind is stilled and the merger "within" occurs. It is a time when you just "be" with God.

How can you do it? There are hundreds of books written on meditation, and I suppose if you weren't so sick, you might find enough time to read them.

Meditation

However, the most helpful idea for me has been: follow your breath. This is to say that you attempt to still your mind and place all of your concentration on your breathing. If you have never tried this before, it means just mentally watching your breath rise and fall. Don't think about anything else except your breath as it moves up and down, in and out. If a thought tries to get in the way of your breath, and believe me, it will, just push the thought gently away and go back to following your breath. As your practice this, you will find that a calmness will begin to fill your mind, replacing any fears that have been there. Don't worry about how the peaceful feelings are happening; just rest in them. One of the biggest problems we have with enjoying the presence of God is trying to figure out how it all works.

Krishnamurti wrote that "meditation is not the means to an end. It is both the means and the end." This is saying that as you practice meditating, good things will happen in the practice itself. It is not as if you arrive someplace so that you can say you have successfully meditated, Rather, as you follow your breath and still your thoughts, something incredibly wonderful happens to you.

Another idea that has been helpful to many people is the use of guided meditations. These are thoughts which guide you to another time and place where you felt safe or at peace. Sometimes revisiting those safe places can be a tremendous peace-filled exerience. If you are uncertain as to how to do this, there are books with meditative ideas and guided images that might be helpful to you. I have listed some of them at the end of this book, so that if you truly are interested in trying new approaches, ask someone to pick up the book for you and try these

If I Should Wake Before I Die

exercises yourself. You can even use a small cassette tape player to record your own meditation exercises so you can listen to your own voice guiding you to peaceful and tranquil places.

Finally, do not be discouraged if you find yourself drifting, and your thoughts overtaking you. Meditation gets easier with practice. Try it three or four times a day and see if one time is better than another. And don't judge yourself if you get distracted by the air conditioner or telephone. John Donne wrote in the sixteenth century, "I throw myself down in my chamber and I call in and invite God and his angels thither, and when they are there, I neglect God and his Angels, for the noise of a fly, for the rattling of a coach, or the whining of a door."

Above all else, remember that you are about the business of inviting God to fill your heart with his Peace and love. Don't be afraid to ask for that as you begin to still your mind and slow those incredibly rushing thoughts. Remember that He is within you, and the only barrier to His joy is your own fearful mind.

DEEP ROOTS

Some say that my teaching is nonsense.
Others call it lofty but impractical.
But to those who have looked inside themselves,
This nonsense makes perfect sense.
And to those who put it into practice,
This loftiness has roots that go deep.

Lao-Tzu

Meditation

LOOKING INSIDE

If you look for the truth outside yourself,
it gets farther and farther away.
Today, walking alone,
I meet him everywhere I step.
He is the same as me, Yet I am not him.
Only if you understand it
in this way will you merge
with the way things are.

Tung-Shan 807-869

A CALM MIND

Lord, my mind is not noisy with desires,
and my heart has satisfied its longing.
 I do not care about religion
or anything that is not you.
I have soothed and quieted my soul
like a child at its mother's breast.
My soul is as peaceful as a child
sleeping in its mother's arms.

Psalm 131

If I Should Wake Before I Die

THE PRESENCE OF GOD

I believe that the best manner
of meditation is as follows:
When, by an act of living faith
you are placed in the Presence of God,
recollect some truth wherein
there is substance and food.
Pause sweetly and gently on it,
not to employ the reason
but merely to calm and fix the mind.
For you must observe
that your principal exercise
Should always be the Presence of God.

Madame Guyon,
A Method of Prayer, 1685

GOD INSIDE US

The seed of God is in us.
Now, the seed of a pear tree
grows into a pear tree.
And a hazel seed grows into a hazel tree.
A seed of God grows into God…
God is a being beyond being
and a Nothingness beyond being.
The most beautiful thing
which a person can say about God
would be for that person
to remain silent from the wisdom
of an inner wealth.

So, be silent,
and quit flapping your gums about God.

Meister Eckhart

Nighttime

Reconcile yourself to wait in this darkness
as long as is necessary, but still go on
longing after Him whom you love.
For if you are to feel Him in this life,
it must always be in this cloud
in this Darkness.

The Cloud of Unknowing

If I Should Wake Before I Die

There was a time in my life when I wanted to be a music teacher. I studied and trained hard, working at developing a rather thin tenor voice into something more credible. To graduate with some degree of acceptance, I had to appear in a voice recital. The song which was chosen for me to sing was entitled "Night." I remember little about the song except the last line which said, "Night is the shadow of God!" Unfortunately, as beautiful as the words were, the music went higher and higher while my voice screeched thinly into the rafters.

On that day, "Night" won.

When you're staring at your own death, Night seems to have a power all of its own. There's just something about the dark which brings out superstition and fear in all of us. It's a scary time.

I suppose, for many of us, the struggle with Night goes way back into our childhood. Perhaps it was those times, following a bad dream, when we laid in the dark looking anxiously around the room. Or those times when spooky stories were told which reflected on things which go "bump in the night."

In my own life, there was a childhood prayer which said "If I should die before I wake, I pray the Lord my soul to take." If you think about it for even a short time, that prayer falls far short of comfort. Especially when you think you might not see the dawn of another day!

Many patients struggle with the Night.

Maybe it's the dark. Or centuries of folktales and mysteries. Regardless, Nighttime is hard for most dying people. Certainly it's a time when the mind runs rampant with fuzzy or frightening thoughts which will be seen with far greater clarity with the

Nighttime

rising of the sun.

We think the worst in the Night.

Consider the words of William Trogdon who said, "Beware thoughts that come in the Night. They aren't turned properly; they come in askew, free of sense and restriction, deriving from the most remote of sources."

It seems as though Night is seen through negative eyes. So, to unlock this unpleasant vision, the darkness must be seen in a new light, no pun intended.

Have you considered the miracle of a seed which leaps to new life from the dark? Or the newborn who emerges from the warm darkness of the womb? Good things often happen in the dark. For decades all of your organs have functioned wonderfully well without even a trace of light.

The day does not have a monopoly on God. His spirit wanders through the Night with equal love and comfort. Nevertheless it is fear which seems to run rampant through the dark, bringing terror to racing minds. The truth of the matter is that we are afraid something horrid will happen during the dark. In anticipation of this, we pull the covers over our heads. Somehow or other, the Light of God which shines into the darkness seems lost in our terror.

However, it is not the Night which hides the peace of God, it is your mind. Fear robs the mind of its ability to rest in God's love. A literal thief in the Night, fear carries you into the imagination of wild, unpredictable possibilities. Alfred Hitchcock, that master of terror, stated his understanding of this dilemma when he said, "There is no terror in a bang, only in the anticipation of it."

If I Should Wake Before I Die

Changing Night fears into peace calls for feeding new sentences to your mind. When the frightening thoughts begin playing their tune in the dark, say to yourself, "I am resting in the arms of God." Or, "The Lord is my shepherd, I am not afraid." You probably will have to repeat those sentences over and over before your mind will absorb the message.

To change feelings calls for a changing of thoughts. Saying comforting words to yourself is a way to walk to the other side of fear. Or asking someone you love to say them for you. It is even helpful to record a whole series of affirming statements which you can listen to if the Night becomes difficult.

Meister Eckhart said, "We are swimming in the womb of God." What a comforting thought in the Night. The fact is that you will either wake up to the light of day or to the smile of God. In that thought there can be no loss.

Pleasant dreams.

THE SILENCE OF THE NIGHT

How absolute and omnipotent
is the silence of the Night!
And yet the stillness seems almost audible —
From all the measureless depths
of air around us, comes a half sound,
a half whisper, as if we could hear the
crumbling and falling away of earth
and all created things in the great miracle
of nature, decay and reproduction
ever beginning, never ending —
the gradual lapse and running of the sand
in the great hourglass of time.

Longfellow

Nighttime

THE LIGHT IN SLEEP

When now he falls asleep;
he takes from this all-comprehending universe
the timber, cuts it down, and himself builds up
of it his own light, by virtue of his own brilliance;
when therefore he sleeps
this spirit serves as light for itself.

Upanishad, IV. 3,9

SOMEWHERE ELSE

All day I think about it, then at night I say it.
Where did I come from, and what am
I supposed to be doing? I have no idea.
My soul is from elsewhere, I'm sure of that,
and I intend to end up there.

Rumi, *Safa Anthology,*
Moyne-Barks translation

BEYOND VISION

We pray that we may come into this Darkness
which is beyond light, and, without seeing
and without knowing, see and to know that
which is above vision and knowledge.

Dionysius, *Mystical Theology*

DAZZLING DARKNESS

There is in God — some say —
A deep, but dazzling darkness;
as men here say it is late and dusky,
because they see not all clear.
O for that Night! Where I in Him
Might live invisible and dim!

Henry Vaughn, "The Night"

If I Should Wake Before I Die

COMFORT IN THE NIGHT

I cry aloud to God; I cry aloud and He hears me.
In times of trouble I pray to the Lord;
all night long I lift my hands in prayer
but I struggle to find comfort.
When I think of God, I sigh;
When I meditate, I feel discouraged.
He keeps me awake all night;
I am so worried that I cannot speak.
I think of days gone by
and remember years of long ago.
I spend the night in deep thought,
I meditate, and this is what I ask myself:
"Has the Lord stopped loving us?"

And then I remember,
Everything you do, O God, is Holy.
…You are the God who works miracles.

Psalm 77:1-6, 8, 11, 13

Pain

Pain is the price
God putteth upon all things.

James Howell

If I Should Wake Before I Die

I once attended a conference on Suffering presented by Stephen Levine, one of the finest teachers in Death and Dying. "Pain is a given in life," he said, "You suffer to the degree that you resist that thought."

Never having thought about it in those terms, I used the next few days to contemplate those words.

I found that I could only agree.

There isn't anyone I know who hasn't formed a somewhat intimate relationship with pain. And those who have tried to avoid the relationship, meet up with pain anyway.

It is part of the price we pay for being human.

Muscles, bones, and tissues eventually break down. There is no escaping this fact, unpleasant or as disagreeable as the thought may be. Pain generally accompanies breakdown, no matter how hard we try to straight-arm it into another direction.

> *Nothing begins and nothing ends*
> *That is not paid with moan.*
> *For we are born in other's pain,*
> *And perish in our own.*

So wrote Francis Thompson back in 1890. This verse is neither positive nor hopeful, but it is, I suspect, realistic.

There is a great tendency to try to sugar-coat pain with some syrupy nonsense about never receiving more than we can bear, or the marvelous lessons that pain can teach us. While this may be a fine subject for a theological debate or a Sunday school class, it is not helpful stuff when you're dying.

To be assured that you will not hurt beyond your capacity to handle it, while at the same time your stomach is swollen to the size of a watermelon,

Pain

and you're so constipated that you can barely breathe, doesn't cut the mustard. Pain is pain! It hurts and does a number on your body, mind, and emotions.

The questions that race through your mind when the pain is escalating focus on: How much longer can I stand this? Will it get worse? And if it gets worse, will I be able to stand it then? And if I can't stand it, then what will happen? At that moment you are not thinking of the beauty of a universe which uses pain to point to that part of you which needs attention.

The fact is that regardless of how bad the pain is, you will have to endure it. Yes, there are pain medications that will help, some better than others. Yes, people will be there to hold your hand. And it is true that meditation and deep breathing helps sometimes, if you are able to take deep breaths.

Nevertheless, you walk through this pain with only the spirit of God to help you. And while you may receive some comfort in that thought, it does little for burning nerves and shortness of breath. There are those who teach the possibility of "softening" around the pain, of imaging love and light around the discomfort; and for those able to do that, this brings a love-relief of its own. Again I would recommend some of Stephen Levine's guided meditations for help with this approach. I have listed some of his writings in the bibliography at the end of this book.

There is at least one comforting thought in the struggle of pain, and that is the knowledge that it will eventually pass. And if it is possible to embrace God's spirit while in the midst of the hurt, the pain may pass sooner. And you will be able to stand it because you simply have no choice.

If I Should Wake Before I Die

For most of us, pain is a part of the movement from this life to the next. So feel great permission to cry out to God in pain and anger. Curse if you need to — God will handle it, and it may make you feel better. Ask questions about why and "how come" but don't expect answers.

Reach up for the invisible hand of the Divine stretching toward you at all times, and even if you can't feel His fingers wrap about yours, hold on tight, scream, and wait for him to pull you over.

There is a calm after the raging storm. And it will be your day in the sun!

A CRY FOR HELP

Lord, God, my savior, I cry out all day,
and at night, I come before you.
Hear my prayer; listen to my cry for help!

So many troubles have fallen on me,
that I am close to death.
I am like all others who are about to die;
all my strength is gone.

You have caused my friends to abandon me;
you have made me repulsive to them.
I am closed in and cannot escape;
my eyes are weak from suffering.
Lord, every day I call to you
and lift my hands to you in prayer.
Is your constant love spoken of in the grave
or your faithfulness in the place of darkness?
Are your miracles seen in that place of darkness,
or your goodness in the land of the forgotten?

From Psalm 88

Pain

CHICKPEA TO COOK

A chickpea* leaps almost over the rim
of the pot where it's being boiled.

"Why are you doing this to me?"

The cook knocks him down with the ladle.

"Don't you try to jump out. You think
I'm torturing you. I'm giving you flavor,
so you can mix with spices and rice
and be the lovely vitality of a human being.

Remember, when you drank rain
in the garden. That was for this."

Grace first. Sexual pleasure,
then a boiling new life begins,
and the Friend† has something good to eat.

Eventually the chickpea will say to the cook,
"Boil me some more. Hit me with
the skimming spoon. I can't do this by myself.
I'm like an elephant that dreams of gardens
and doesn't pay attention to his driver.
You're my Cook, my Driver, my way into
Eternal Existence. I love your cooking."

The Cook says, "I was once like you,
fresh from the ground. Then I boiled in Time,
and boiled in the Body, two fierce boilings.
My animal soul grew powerful. I controlled it
with practices, and boiled some more,
and boiled once beyond that,
and became your TEACHER."

Rumi, Translation by Coleman Banks

* Rumi writes of our lives being "boiled"
   to perfection much like the chickpea, being
   cooked to perfection as a process of healing.

† The Friend is the Spirit living within.

143

If I Should Wake Before I Die

THE NEW HEAVEN AND EARTH

*Then I saw a new heaven and a new earth,
the First heaven and the first earth
disappeared, and the sea vanished.
And I saw the Holy City, the new Jerusalem
coming down out of heaven from God,
prepared and ready, like a bride dressed
to meet her husband.*

I heard a loud voice speaking from the throne:

*"Now God's home is with humankind.
He will live with them,
and they shall be his people.
God himself will be with them
and be their God.
He will wipe away all tears from their eyes.
There will be no more death,*

*no more grief, or crying or Pain.
The old things have disappeared."*

*Then the one who sits on the throne said, "And
now I make all things new."*

Revelation 21: 1-5

ON THE CROSS

My God, My God, why hast thou Forsaken Me?

Psalm 22; The Words of Jesus

A NATURAL DEATH

*I ask for a natural death,
no teeth on the ground, no blood about the place...*

*It's not death I fear,
but unspecified, unlimited pain.*

Robert Lowell

Powerlessness

My grace is all you need,
for my power is greatest
when you are weak.

2 Corinthians 12:10

If I Should Wake Before I Die

A patient once told me, "You have no idea how it feels to not have enough strength to brush your own teeth." I had to admit he was right. After all, I had just bounced up the steps to his second floor bedroom without giving it a thought. "Not being able to control your own body is a terrible position to be in," he said. "It makes me feel totally out of control. And I hate it."

Leaving his house, I started to reflect on his words. Control is such a big issue in all of our lives. I certainly could see it at work in my own. From trying to control my environment, crowded with uncooperative young adults, to attempting to keep my cholesterol in line, I specialize in control. "Control is one of your best things," says my wife.

The problem is that it doesn't work.

Control is an addictive issue in the lives of most people. It mirrors the insecurity of the world we live in. If only we could have some guarantees about how things are going to come out, we might be able to relax a bit on the control stuff.

The trouble is, however, that life offers no guarantees, and we know it!

Bad things do happen to good people, and just because you brush with fluoride doesn't mean you won't get cavities. Exercise does not mean you won't die; neither does 2000 units of vitamin C each day.

The truth is that control and fear walk closely together in life. The more unsafe you feel about something, the more important it will be for you to try to control that area of your world.

Feeling powerless to prevent something bad from happening is one of the worst experiences you may

Powerlessness

have to endure. You know, better than most, about the feelings of helplessness that surface in life. The dying process is a classroom in powerlessness. It forces you into an uncontrollable position.

Unfortunately, the only way to the other side of powerlessness is through surrender. And although surrender sometimes gets bad press, in reality it is a decision of power, not weakness. When you surrender, it is always through a choice you make to stop trying to control what is happening, and instead ride the wave to the next stop.

Surrender does not mean you will die tomorrow, it has nothing to do with time. It means that you are halting your fight with control, choosing instead to rest in the Spirit higher than yourself.

Surrender is a power word. It simply says that you recognize there is a higher way to approach your situation, namely allowing the flow of God to carry you where you cannot lift yourself.

Recently I was driving on extremely icy roads, slipping and sliding with each turn or acceleration. What I learned was to avoid using the brakes each time I started to slide for that only made matters worse. Rather, if I took my foot off the accelerator when beginning to skid and resisted the impulse to slam on the brakes, I flowed straight through the icy spot.

This is how it is with powerlessness. The more you resist, the more you slide off the road. Loss of control is nothing new to any of us, we never had it. Sadly, we just acted as though we did.

Surrender to the power and nurturing love of God has always been an option. When we have a fair amount of body strength, we tend to avoid that

If I Should Wake Before I Die

choice. Now that you are in a position which points to the sensibleness of "letting God do it," why not take your foot off the brake and let Him steer.

Perhaps you can take a nap in the back seat; the rest will feel wonderful and the trip will suddenly become more pleasant.

DIVINE ASSISTANCE

We should keep up in our hearts
a constant sense of our own weakness,
not with a design to discourage the mind and
depress the spirits,
but with a view to drive us
out of ourselves in search
of the Divine assistance.

Hannah More

REST

And Jesus said,
"Come unto me all of you
who are carrying heavy loads,
and I will give you rest.
Take my yoke and put it on you,
and learn from me, because
I am gentle and humble in spirit.
For the yoke I will give you is easy,
and the load I will put on you is light."

Matt. 11:28

Powerlessness

IN HIS HANDS

*God holds your future as He holds your past
and present. They are one to Him, and so
they should be one to you. Yet in this world
the temporal progression still seems real.
And so you are not asked to understand
the lack of sequence really found in time.*

*You are best asked to let the future go and
place it in God's hands. And you will see
by your experience that you have laid the past
and present in His hands as well, because
the past will punish you no more,
and future dread will not be meaningless.
Release the future. For the past is gone and
what is present, freed from its bequest of grief*

*and misery, of pain and loss, becomes the
instant in which time escapes the bondage
of illusions where it runs its pitiless,
inevitable course.*

A Course In Miracles, Lesson 194

THE GARDEN

*If you aren't headed briskly
toward that garden,
then get rid of your congestion
and smell the fragrance.
Let it draw your soul to the garden.*

Rumi

149

If I Should Wake Before I Die

I REST IN GOD

I rest in God. This thought
will bring to you the rest and quiet,
peace and stillness, and the safety
and the happiness you seek.
I rest in God. This thought has the power
to wake the sleeping truth in you, whose vision
sees beyond appearances to the same truth
in everyone and everything there is.
Here is the end of suffering for all the world.
I rest in God... There is no suffering
this thought cannot heal.

A Course In Miracles: Lesson 109

Prayer

Prayer is neither
word nor gesture.
Chant nor sound.
It is to be
in still communication
with our Ground.

Angelus Silesius

If I Should Wake Before I Die

Prayer is connection with God.

Everything else is a matter of approach, style, and theology. Some people get on their knees to pray, some just lie in bed. There are those who say wonderful words in prayer, while others can only manage to repeat childhood memories.

Almost everyone looks for an answer.

The tricky part of prayer is that there are no answers, at least none which satisfy. Instead there is only a uniting of your spirit with the Great Spirit. And in this is found peace, joy, and the experience of love.

Prayer is a reaching out to touch your Source so that comfort can be found. It is not unlike the stretching of a baby animal toward its mother. In the warmth and presence of the parent is safety and satisfaction.

When you pray, your arms meet the ever-present Force of God which continually surrounds you. All prayer does is open your emotional body to receive and enjoy God's love and devotion. It is not a matter of the right words or form, rather prayer is rooted in your desire for unity with the Protector of your life.

Sometimes it is impossible to even express your wish for joining with God. Your pain may be too great to focus on such a desire. Or your weariness too great to remain awake long enough to voice your hope for Union.

It really doesn't matter how you communicate your desire for God's protective arms of love. An internal wish is as great a prayer as an organized speech. This is what John Bunyan meant when he wrote, "The best prayers have often more

Prayer

groans than words."

Unfortunately, there are those persons who worry that because they didn't pray when they felt well, it is somehow hypocritical to pray when faced with death.

The fact is that it doesn't matter when you decide to reach for God. There are no rules or scorecards kept on your prayer time, and the love of your Great Parent does not worry about where you've been in the past. A simple prayer that expresses your desire for the embracing by God is eagerly heard and accepted since His arms are already around you. What prayer does is allow you to feel God's love, and in that Divine hug to receive peace and comfort.

So, try not to get caught on all the old stuff about prayer. You are struggling enough these days to walk with courage and boldness toward your Address change, without spending any more energy judging your past behaviors. It doesn't matter if it takes a terminal illness to bring you to experience the Union with God. Rejoice in the marriage that occurs between you and your Creator instead of chewing over the dry bones of the past.

Pray or groan or weep or meditate or reach out. It's all the same to a loving and caring God who hears all and fills your heart with nurturing and peace.

Enjoy the Creator who cradles you tonight.

PURPOSE

To let go into Oneness
is the purpose of true prayer.

Polly Berrien Berends

If I Should Wake Before I Die

OUR FATHER

And Jesus said, …"Pray then like this:
Our Father who art in Heaven
Hallowed be thy name.
Thy kingdom come, Thy will be done,
On earth as it is in heaven.
Give us this day our daily bread;
And forgive us our debts,
As we also have forgiven our debtors;
And lead us not into temptation,
But deliver us from evil."

DIVINE UNITY

Jalalu'l Din was asked, "Is there any way
to God nearer than the ritual prayer?"
"No", he replied; "but prayer does not consist
in forms alone. Formal prayer has a beginning
and an end, like all forms and bodies and
everything that partakes of speech and sound;
but the soul is unconditioned and infinite…
Absorption in the Divine Unity
is the soul of prayer."

Fihi ma fihi, R. A. Nicholson

Prayer

CALLING HOME

You pray by touching the deepest part of you,
that longs, that needs, that Is.
Let it speak in its own language,
more often than not without words.

The longing itself is the prayer of life.
"I want to be with you again, God.
I want to be Home."
There is no how to prayer. It simply is.
It is part of the Oneness.
It is a part of your coming Home.
Do it whatever way you like.

Prayer is to assure you
of your connection with Home.
I'm sure you remember it —
when you had to call home
just to be sure it was there.
Prayer is like that. It is calling Home.

Emmanuel

LONGING

Prayer is not asking.
It is a longing of the soul.
It is daily admission of one's weakness…
It is better in prayer
to have a heart without words
than words without a heart.

Gandhi

155

If I Should Wake Before I Die

GOD IS HERE

In the presence of god,
there is nothing left for which to pray…
Your whole prayer becomes
a continuous song of gratitude
that God is love, that God is here,
and that God is now…
Prayer thereby becomes
a recognition of God's presence,
a communion with God,
a resting back in God's bosom,
a holding of God's hand,
a feeling of the Divine presence.
That is prayer and nothing else.

Joel Goldsmith, *Leave Your Nets*

SINCERITY

One "Hail Mary" uttered sincerely
is more potent and better than
a thousand uttered mechanically,
for the heart is not made pure by prayer
but rather prayer is made pure
by the pure heart.
…When I pray for something, I do not pray;
When I pray for nothing, I really pray.
…To pray for anything except God
might be called idolatry or injustice.

Meister Eckhart

156

Receiving

Only those who have,
receive.

Joseph Roux

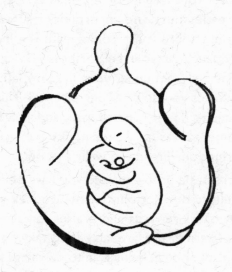

If I Should Wake Before I Die

One of the toughest parts of dying is the struggle to accept your feelings of dependency. Beyond the pain, restlessness, and uncertainty that each new day brings, there is the coping with the increasing consequences of your helplessness. Dying knocks the pins out from under you; it, as my father used to say, takes you down a "peg or two." Things that you used to do for yourself easily suddenly become monumental tasks. Reaching for a magazine or buttering your bread can wear you out.

This creates a problem since you have been raised in a culture that not only encourages self-sufficiency, but offers rewards and praises for being so. If you're like me, you probably have taken a certain amount of pride in being able to do things yourself, to look after your own needs. And now, it's not so easy to give up your own self-care.

The dying process creates difficulties for the muscles and sinews of your body. Simply put, you just can't continue to do what you have always done; you don't have the strength. Not only does this realization whack away at your need for control of your own life, it also means that you have to find a way to become comfortable with somebody doing for you what you have always done for yourself.

Rarely does anyone handle this dilemma gracefully. First of all, you're scared; secondly, you're angry at all of this dying business anyway; and third, you don't want to trade your self-sufficiency in for the care of someone else, regardless of how loving and kind they might be.

Almost everyone has a difficult time with receiving. There's lots of reasons for this and not enough space to write about it. Suffice it to say that few

Receiving

people want to be dependent on others, it costs too much; and the vulnerability is enormous. Back in 1752, Thomas Fuller, a physician, wrote that "there is a bitterness in a gift since it deprives us of our liberty." True or not, this is a worry for many people. Receiving from others can lead to feelings of unworthiness, dependency, and even anger. "We do not quite forgive a giver," Emerson said, "the hand that feeds us is in some danger of being bitten."

When you have to depend on someone else to do for you those things you so easily did before, it is a reminder of the continual movement of the dying process. With each little thing that you are forced to release comes more dependency, and perhaps more fear. Beyond this, there is the incredible rage at placing someone you love in the position of having to take care of you. Not only can this lead to your worrying about the physical and emotional cost to them, it is absolutely not the way you want it to be, nor what you are accustomed to, in any manner.

I remember a woman patient, who was so used to caretaking her family, that she panicked when she realized that Thanksgiving was coming and she might not be strong enough to prepare the turkey (with her own special stuffing) and her husband's favorite mince pie. In an act of final effort, she had her hospital bed moved into the dining room and directed the entire meal from her propped pillows. By Christmas, she had to allow herself to receive dinner from the very capable hands of her adult children. This was extremely hard for her to allow, but the movement of her disease and the weakness of her body, forced the decision.

What she missed in this painful struggle was the

powerful gift that she gave to her daughters by "allowing" them to give to her. This provided a tiny piece of "giving back" to their mother, a self-sacrificing woman, who had spent her life in "doing" for her husband and children.

Receiving is hard work, and work is exactly what it is. For most of you, receiving is foreign territory and perhaps it needs a new vision, a different way of looking at it. Perhaps you might view receiving as a way of "giving" to those who wish to take care of you. By releasing your resistance to it, and graciously accepting from the loving care-givers in your life, you are giving to them a gift beyond any you can imagine. To wash my father's body, and to swab out his mouth when he was unable to do those things for himself, became a gift to me. As one of his caregivers, his receptivity turned into my blessing.

Receiving, then, becomes a giving to others in your life, as well as a giving to yourself as you accept more of the "letting go" process of life.

There is one more thought about receiving that seems important to me. From a spiritual perspective, you are not alone where you are in your dying process. God has been leading you throughout, holding you close. And now, you are at a different point, where blessings can flow to everyone involved in your care. But only if you do not halt the process by a refusal to accept your limitations. This business of dying is a chance for inner healing for everyone involved, not just you. Caregivers are spiritually fed by the opportunities you allow. Dying is truly a team sport.

It is, you see, God, you, your soul, and your loving caregivers who come together in your dying journey. To deny anyone his or her chances to give and receive is to short-circuit the trip.

Receiving

Receiving is giving to everyone. Lie back and thrill to it!

GIFTS

Be prepared at all times for the gifts of God
and be ready always for new ones.
For God is a thousand times
more ready to give than we are to receive.

As God is omnipotent in his deeds,
so too the soul is equally profound
in its capacity to receive.

Meister Eckhart

FROM ABOVE

Every good gift and every perfect gift
is from above.

James 1:17

AN OPEN MIND

A good traveler has not fixed plans
and is not intent upon arriving.
A good artist lets his intuition
lead him wherever it wants.
A good scientist has freed himself of concepts
and keeps his mind open to what is.
Thus the Master is available to all people
and he doesn't reject anyone.
He is ready to use all situations
and doesn't waste anything.
This is called embodying the light.

Lao-Tzu

If I Should Wake Before I Die

A CALLING

Just as we are called to serve others,
others are called to serve us.
Sometimes it is a greater challenge
to accept another's love and assistance
than it is to offer our own service.

Molly Young Brown

GIVING OF YOURSELF

Whenever you give to one person
you are giving to all.
Whenever you give to a brother
you are giving to yourself.
There is no slight act of thoughtfulness;
every act of kindness is supremely powerful.

Alan Cohen

A PRAYER

God of all creation,
grant us this day some meeting
with bird or moon, sheep or star,
insect or the sun itself;
that we might marvel and know our place
and praise you again and for ever and ever.

Gabe Huck

Receiving

DON'T POSTPONE YOUR YES

Muhammed is said to have said,
"Whoever belongs to God, God belongs to."
A drop of water constantly fears
that it may evaporate into air,
or be absorbed by the ground.
It doesn't want to be used up in those ways,
but when it lets go and falls
into the ocean it came from,
it finds protection from the other deaths.
Its droplet form is gone,
but its watery essence has become
vast and inviolable.

Listen to me, friends, because you are a drop,
and you can honor yourselves in this way.
What could be luckier than to have
the Ocean come to court the drop?

For God's sake, Don't postpone your yes!
Give up, and become the giver.

Rumi
Translation: Coleman Barks

If I Should Wake Before I Die

Religion

Religion is not what
you will get after reading
all the scriptures of the world.
It is not really what
is grasped by the brain.
It is a heart grasp.

Gandhi
New Chronicle obituary, Jan. 31, 1948

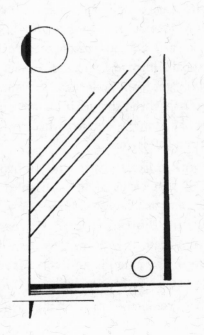

If I Should Wake Before I Die

My first major crime heist occurred when I was but eight years old. My grandfather, unknowingly acted as my "lookout man," while I ran into my neighbor's back yard on the pretense of reclaiming my lost baseball. Instead I entered a small cabin and stole a flashlight from underneath a bunk. Later I placed the flashlight in the grass behind our garage where I would "stumble" upon it while my father and I were cutting the lawn.

It worked like a charm, and though my father was highly suspicious of how a flashlight found its way into our yard, I now had one of my very own. Even though I thoroughly enjoyed reading under the covers at night with my new flashlight, I eventually gave in to my guilt and confessed to the entire incident.

What I remember most of that experience was the vision I had as I "hid" the flashlight in the grass next to the garage. For one brief shining moment, I saw God watching me. Indeed, He was an awesome sight, leaning over the roof of the garage to see me bury that flashlight in the high grass. His eyes flashed and he had long fingers that pointed towards me. What I remember most vividly, however, was his dramatic bald head! For some reason, the God of my childhood was bald.

Decades later, when I try to imagine God looking at me, I still see the bald-headed, narrow-eyed Deity peering at me as I crouched beside the garage. As I have thought about this experience and the ways in which I remember God, I also recall the Sunday School classes where I learned about this ever-watching Divine Investigator.

"He who keepeth Israel neither slumbers nor

Religion

sleeps," my teacher used to say. And of course, Santa Claus had some of those attributes in that he "saw me when I slept and when I was awake." Santa also kept a list. I quickly mixed up my Religion with my culture, and then, for good measure, threw in my father's ever watchful eye as he caught me in one lie after another. Mixed together this became my Religion and my view of God.

It is my suspicion that you, too, have a Religion of mixed ingredients. You might recall the teachings from your childhood which may have frightened you more than provided comfort. Added to that, you may remember the remarks of parents and grandparents about God, heaven, hell, and disasters. I remember being told by a seamstress that if you "sewed on Sunday, you would have to take the stitches out with your nose in the afterlife." Thank God, I never sewed. My grandmother told me that God cared about my appearance, and my grandfather said that my lost cat went to kitty heaven. In first grade, one of my friend's father died because God needed him to lead a choir in heaven. At least, that was the word around the classroom.

Is it any wonder that by the time life throws its incredible curve balls at you, there is total confusion as to how to draw comfort from your Religion. When you were told by your doctors about your disease, and the fact that nothing else could be done, were you able to draw on your Religion for consolation and encouragement? Did you raise the usual questions of why and why not? What about your answers? Did they provide satisfaction or comfort?

It seems to me that when faced with life's crises,

If I Should Wake Before I Die

most people return to the religious legacies of child-hood. Perhaps this is because during childhood was the first time you may have heard about death and dying, or heaven and hell. Many times early religious teachings were used to frighten children into good behavior. Unfortunately, the lessons of an angry or revengeful God do not contribute to the sense of inner peace that everyone is searching for. Nor do old stories of half truths help when you're faced with a cancer that is racing through your body.

Also, many people learn that Religion is a matter of exclusiveness, that "my" Religion is **THE** Religion. Henry Fielding in Tom Jones writes, "When I mention Religion, I mean the Christian Religion; not only the Christian Religion but the Protestant Religion; and not only the Protestant Religion but the Church of England."

How can you draw on the strengths and beauty of your Religion to carry you through the dark night of the soul with these limited and parochial teachings? Is it possible for you to find the truth and comfort provided in your Religion at this time in your dying process?

My guess is the answer is yes, but only if you erase the childhood teachings that may be rooted in superstitions and half-truth tales, and replace them with the rich, deep comfort that every Religion holds. For example, God is **NOT** a bald-headed spy checking up on me for each indiscretion, and then doling out punishments at his every whim. God is the Source in which I am rooted and connected, who holds me in His love and oneness so that I will never be alone or separated.

At this time in your journey as you struggle with the meaning of life while facing death, it is so very

Religion

important to put away your "concepts" of God and to embrace his spirit within. Austin O'Malley wrote, "Religion is a process of turning your skull ino a tabernacle, not of Going up to Jerusalem once a year."

Many patients tell me they are not religious. What most of them mean by that is that they are not "churched" or "institutionalized." It is rare that I meet anyone who does not have a belief in a Creative Source which sustains life. Being religious does not mean that you quote scripture or have perfect attendance pins from Bible School decorating your walls. Instead, being religious more accurately approaches an internal meeting with God. "We give people a dose of Religion," wrote Kenneth Pillar, in a letter to Margaret Pepper, "when they are looking for an encounter with the Living God."

At this time in your life, when time is precious and your need for support and comfort great, why not turn toward the deep promises of your religious roots. All Religions offer great hope and encouragement. Forget all the details and grab on to the good stuff. You can drop all the harsh judgments, too, and anchor yourself to the notion of total forgiveness. That's what will carry you through the tough days.

Arnold Patton writes, "What you focus on expands." I can think of no greater place to put your focus than on the loving, grace-filled, forgiving God of your Religion. Let that idea expand throughout your whole being until you are floating on Holy Ground. Remember, you will never sink for you are being held by the loving arms of your Creator.

GOD'S SONG OF RELIGION

There is Religion in everything around us,
a calm and holy Religion in all we look upon.
It is a meek and blessed influence, flowing
gently upon the heart. It comes quietly,
and without excitement; it has no terror and
no gloom; it is untrammelled by creeds.
It is written on the arched sky; it looks out
from every star. It is on the sailing clouds
and in the invisible wind; it is among the hills
and valleys of the earth. It is spread out like
a legible language upon the broad face of an
unsleeping ocean; it calls softly to the heart
that is open to hear. It uplifts the spirit within us,
and awakens us to a world of beauty and holiness.
It is God's song, that flows through all creation.

John Ruskin, from *Earth Prayers*

LOOKING FOR GOD

Are you looking for me?
I am in the next seat.
My shoulder is against yours.
You will not find me in stupas (towers),
not in Indian shrine rooms,
nor in synagogues, nor in cathedrals;
not in masses, nor kirtans,
not in legs winding around your own neck,
nor in eating nothing but vegetables.
When you really look for me,
you will see me instantly —
you will find me in the tiniest house of time.
Kabir says: Student, tell me what is God?
He is the breath inside the breath.

Kabir, Translation by Robert Bly

170

Religion

THE ONE GOD

Truth is one; sages call it by various names,
It is one sun which reflects in all ponds.
It is the one water
which slakes the thirst of all;
It is the one air which sustains all life.
It is the one fire which shines in all houses.
Colors of the cows may be different
but milk is white.
Flowers and bees may be different,
but honey is the same.
Systems of faith may be different,
but God is One.
As the rain dropping from the sky
wends its way toward the ocean,
So the prayers offered in all faiths
reach the one God, who is supreme.

From the Rig Veda (Hindu Scriptures)

MERCY, NOT SACRIFICE

…Let us try to know the Lord.
He will come to us as surely as the day dawns,
as surely as the spring rains fall upon the earth.

But the Lord says, "Israel and Judah,
what am I going to do with you?
Your love for me disappears as quickly as
morning mist; it is like dew, that vanishes
early in the day. That is why I have sent
my prophets to you with my message
of judgment and destruction.

What I want from you is plain and clear:
I want your constant love, not your animal
sacrifices. I desire mercy, not sacrifice."

Hosea 6:3-6

THE BEST GIFT

The wonderful sense
that I'm not doing it,
that I'm outside my ego
and am surrendering
my instrumentality
to that power
that is coming through me;
that is, of course,
the best gift
a person can get
from his tradition.

Rabbi Zalman Schacter

Spirituality

We carry within us,

the wonders we seek without us.

Sir Thomas Browne (1642)

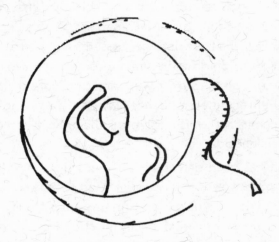

If I Should Wake Before I Die

I remember when Spirituality was one of my least favorite words. Perhaps it was my upbringing in the fundamentalist church that colored the word in a mix with salvation and soul collecting that turned me off to all "spiritual" matters. And, as in most cases, the baby does get tossed away with the bath water. Spiritual became a concept to avoid, and more often to treat with sarcasm. More than once I entertained audiences with my finger-pointing comic act which parroted the evangelists of my childhood.

It has been only in recent times that I have found the beauty in the Spiritual. And to do so meant a new and wondrous journey into the Divine, starting with an innocent question from a hospice director inquiring into the condition of a patient's 'religious pain.' For my part, I had no idea what reli-

gious pain meant, much less was I able to give an intelligent answer to her question. A week later, she changed questions on me: "Do you think this patient is in 'spiritual' pain?" This was a new word which changed everything.

I had never explored the difference between religious and spiritual before. Since then, I have spent considerable time looking at the two concepts, and, indeed, they seem to point to two distinct philosophies. In the chapter on Religion, I have pointed out some of the notions surrounding that term, but basically, it (Religion) has to do with our system of beliefs and behaviors. Built on creeds, dogmas, and teachings, Religion points to our human life and the rules that govern us toward the higher path in God.

Spirituality, on the other hand, points to our relationship with the Creative Source of all life. It is concerned with the connection between ourselves and God.

We live in a culture where there are many "religious" people who are not "spiritual." Equally, there are those who consider themselves "spiritual," that is, they are interested in the relationship with God, but not the structure that supports worship, education, and so forth. And then, of course, there are those who embrace both.

It seems to me that when you are dying, the critical factor has to do with your relationship with God and how you experience it. Since there is no greater aloneness than the feeling of the dying journey, to die feeling such aloneness is an enormous tragedy. When there does not seem to be any grasping hand that carries beyond the physical, the sense of isolation is immense.

So, I suppose the question is: how can you connect with God during the dying process? In a sense, it is an extension of the difficulty of joining with God when you felt healthy. Most of us don't know how to make it happen, and have probably searched for a Heavenly relationship since we were children. The longing to connect with God, it seems to me, is the most profound yearning of life.

My sense is that you are probably looking for the right thing in the wrong place. Searching for God "out there" is a fruitless hunt. The results are maddening to say the least. In this attempt to find God, the Eastern term "maya" is an adequate concept of what many folks go through. "Maya" states that your desires are in the right direction but your map is misdrawn.

If I Should Wake Before I Die

God is not "out there" someplace waiting for you to uncover Him. He is not in some secret hiding place which only the saints and religious masters know of, nor is He perched up on some throne watching to see if you are misbehaving. You will not find Him if you have the right password or memorize enough scriptures.

It is not the finding of God that is the key; rather it is the unbelievable discovery that *you are IN God.* Can you understand the humor in all of this? The very God we are searching for is in the air we breathe, the water we drink, and the world in which we live. God flows around us, through us, and between us. Skin does not keep Him "out there" someplace where we can only access him with offerings, attendance, or sacrifice.

Spirituality, you see, is about the business of becoming aware of your partnership in God. **YOU ARE NOT ALONE!** You just "feel that way." Any aloneness you experience on your journey toward the end of your physical life is an aloneness of disbelief. And simply because you "feel" alone does not make it true. A *Course in Miracles* says "the Universe of Love does not stop because you do not see it." God is in your every breath and eye blink. There is no escaping His loving spirit which fills your entire body.

Enlightenment is not about great theological mysteries; it is about "Waking Up" to your partnership in God. And once that happens, you can never be alone again. Oh, of course, you can get scared and feel alone, but such an emotion cannot destroy your knowledge of the constant Divine connection. Once you *KNOW* who you are as an extension of God, no matter how afraid you get, that old dragon can never have the power it once did.

Meister Eckhart's statement "you are swimming in the womb of God," is a perfect description of your condition. It really doesn't matter if you are religious or if you know any scriptures or holy words, since you are held in the Arms of God with every breath. Religious ignorance is no barrier to who you are in God. Prayer doesn't really matter, nor does any Divine record keeper watch your actions to measure their appropriateness, being *IN GOD* transcends all that stuff.

So you see, you are a Spiritual being whether you know it or not. If you've read these words, you now know who you are. And if you choose not to believe it, that's o.k. since you are being held by God regardless of what you believe.

Now, there are those of you who will struggle with these words since you believe in a "conditional God." And that's o.k., also. But please be gentle with yourself and enjoy the love of God which is both forgiving and "grace-filled."

For those of you who are wondering about your spiritual partnership with God, celebrate it with a smile. Tell someone you love that you are not alone anymore, nor have you ever been. And remember, as you move toward your final breaths, you will be totally and lovingly carried by the God in whom you live.

LOOKING WITHIN

Who looks outside dreams —
Who looks inside wakes."

Carl Jung

If I Should Wake Before I Die

GOD IS ALL

God, you can show your great power
any time you wish,
In your sight the whole world is a grain of sand,
barely heavy enough to tip a pair of scales,
a drop of dew on the ground in the morning.
You are powerful enough to do anything
but you are merciful to everyone;
you overlook our sins and give us time to repent.
You love everything that exists;
You do not despise anything you have made.
If you had not liked it,
you would not have made it.
You have allowed it all to exist, O Lord,
because it is yours,
and you love every living thing.
Your immortal spirit is in every one of them.

Wisdom of Solomon, 11

THE WILL OF GOD

Have faith in this one thing,
and it will be sufficient;
God wills you be in Heaven,
and nothing can keep you from it,
or it from you.
Your wildest misperceptions,
your weird imaginings,
your blackest nightmares all mean nothing.
They will not prevail against
the peace God wills for you.
The Holy Spirit will restore your sanity
because insanity is not the will of God.
…The communication link that
God Himself placed with you,
joining your Mind with His cannot be broken."

Course In Miracles, Ch. 13, T. Page 249

Spirituality

GOD INSIDE

Inside this clay jug
there are canyons and pine mountains,
and the maker of canyons and pine mountains!
All seven oceans are inside,
and hundreds of millions of stars.
The acid that tests gold is there,
and the one that judges jewels.
And the music from the strings no one touches,
And the source of all water.
If you want the truth, I will tell you the truth:
Friend, listen, the God whom I love is inside.

Kabir, Translation by Robert Bly

I AM ALWAYS WITH YOU

When I go, you will not be left all alone;
I will come back to you.
In a little while the world will see me no more,
but you will see me, and because I live,
you also will live.
When that day comes,
you will know that I am in my Father
and that you are in me,
just as I am in you.
…Peace is what I leave with you;
it is my own peace that I give you.
I do not give it as the world does.
Do not be worried and upset;
Do not be afraid.

John 14:18-20, 27

If I Should Wake Before I Die

Trust

I would rather work
with God in the dark
than go alone in the light.

Mary Gardiner Brainard
Not Known

If I Should Wake Before I Die

In the film "O God," George Burns, speaking as the Almighty, tells a frightened John Denver, "Trust me, like it says on your money." Easier said than done.

It was over thirty years ago, or so it seems, when my father and I stood together in line waiting to pay for the Sunday paper. We were chuckling about how stupid Charlie Brown was to actually believe that Lucy would hold the football for him to kick, when we all knew that she would pull it away at the last minute. Year after year, we looked for this fall classic, pointing out the many ways in which poor Charlie, wanting to believe so much in Lucy, fell on his gullible back.

Trust is a difficult stint in life, to say nothing of when you're dying. How far trust has carried you may have seemed more a matter of circumstance rather than destiny. Did you "happen" on the right Doctor, or the wrong one? Do you live in an area with multi-medical facilities, or in a rural spot with limited access? How do you know you can trust the counsel of the medical folks or the well meaning relatives with their packages of advice?

Then, of course, there are the countless TV shows and dedicated religious folks telling you about trusting God and the potential for miracles. And it all sounds so good… and hopeful. Yet, there is a lot of confusion and uncertainty. How do you rest in the arms of a Loving Spirit which you have never seen, much less experienced His comfort? Or, how do you know that your Doctor wasn't the one that graduated last in his or her class? Most of us have lived our lives less in line with trust and more in keeping with the Koran, which says, "Trust God, but tie your camel anyway." Or in the words of Finley Peter Dunne, the last century American humorist, who wrote, "Trust every-

Trust

body, but cut the cards."

You learn about trust early on in childhood. And there's not time nor reason in this book to analyze the injuries of childhood and the numerous ways they have impacted your willingness to trust. The fact is that at this ending journey of your physical life, you are backed into a corner, that old familiar spot between a rock and a hard place. Trust no longer becomes a subject for philosophical discussions, or a shaking of heads in the direction of the latest political act of distrust, it now becomes a matter of choice.

In fact, it probably is a "Hobson's Choice." If you're not familiar with that phrase, it comes from a rent-a-horse man, who was somewhat of a forerunner of Hertz and Avis, except he peddled the four-legged modes of transportation. Unfortunately for Mr. Hobson, as his business increased, more and more customers arrived at his home in the early morning hours, in order to choose the best horses to rent. Gradually, he was being wakened in the middle of the night with people wanting to pick the best of his herd. So, Mr. Hobson came up with a creative idea, namely, that he would open at 7:00 A.M. for all customers. However, the night before, he would shift the horses around in their stalls so the same horse would never be in the same stall twice. As customer number one arrived, he got the horse in stall number one. Customer two, was given the horse in stall two, and so on. Gradually, this became known as a Hobson's Choice. It was sort of "no choice at all."

At this time in your life, you are faced with a type of Hobson's choice. You will go through the final weeks and days of your illness whether you like it or not. And at this point, the creative work of the

If I Should Wake Before I Die

medical community will both lead and follow you in pain management and comfort. Family members will be close, and your feelings will be, and certainly already are, intense and difficult. In all of this, you will have a "Hobson's choice" regarding trust.

Believe it or not, it really doesn't matter, because you now squarely rest in the arms of the Universe. What this means and how it will go, no one really knows, especially you. Nevertheless, the die is cast and the journey continues, steering its own course toward the wisdom of God.

As for trust, you can either embrace it or choose not to. The only choice you now have is whether to ride on its back, or refuse to acknowledge that there is anything to hold on to at all. Trust is always a matter of choice in that you can draw comfort from it or not. Obviously, the more you feel upheld

and connected, the less frightening the unknown seems.

It is no surprise that trust and doubt share the same bed. In your fear, those "trustable" beliefs which have provided enormous inner peace during your healthy years, can fade into a dim light of uncertainty. Fear does that to all of us; you're not alone in the terror of the dark. "Lord, I believe. Help thou my unbelief" is not just the cry of an old Christian theologian; it is the prayer of any person who seriously looks at the struggles of living and dying.

So, what can you do? The words of Martin Luther say it for me: "Trust God, and sin on bravely." I have read of the great Spiritual masters speaking of "stepping out off the edge of a cliff, trusting that the Divine hand will catch you." I always assumed they

Trust

were speaking symbolically, although there are those who claim this is a physical promise as well.

Regardless, your turn to "step off" is coming, and so is mine. No one knows when the step will come, and probably most of us need a great deal of nudging. A sign I saw in an office one time showed a photo of the Grand Canyon, at the edge of a tremendous drop into space. Printed below were the words, "Only a fool attempts to leap a precipice in one jump."

Well, guess what? That makes us all fools since the step into space shows no elevator and tangible net. So, stepping out is all that's left. My assurance to you is that you will be caught, whether you think so or not. Like the small child who jumps from the couch into her daddy's arms, *YOU WILL NOT BE DROPPED!*

DOES GOD CARE?

Israel, why then do you complain
that the Lord doesn't know your troubles
or care if you suffer injustice?
Don't you know? Haven't you heard?
The Lord is the everlasting God;
He created all the world.
He never grows tired or weary.
No one understands his thoughts.
He strengthens those who are weak and tired.
Even those who are young grow weak;
young men can fall exhausted.
But those who trust in the Lord for help
will find their strength renewed.
They will rise up on wings like eagles;
they will run and not get weary;
they will walk and not grow weak."

Isaiah 40:27–31

If I Should Wake Before I Die

THE MYSTERY

Eyes look but cannot see it.
Ears listen but cannot hear it.
Hands grasp but cannot touch it.
Beyond the sense lies the great Unity -
Invisible, Inaudible, Intangible.
What rises up appears bright
What settles down appears dark
Yet there is neither darkness nor light
just an unbroken dance of shadows.
From nothingness to fullness
and back again to nothingness.
This formless form, This imageless image,
cannot be grasped by mind or might.

Try to face it
In what place will you stand?
Try to follow it
To what place will you go?
Know That which is beyond all beginnings
And you will know everything right here and now.
Know everything in this moment
And you will know the Eternal Tao.

Tao Te Ching

Trust

DEPENDING

I depend on God alone;
I put my hope in him.
He alone protects and saves me;
He is my defender,
and I shall never be defeated.
My salvation and honor depend on God:
He is my strong protector,
He is my shelter.
Trust in God at all times, my people.
Tell Him all your troubles
for He is our refuge.

Psalm 62: 5-8

DON'T BE AFRAID

This is why I tell you, do not be worried about
the food and drink you need in order to stay alive,
or about the clothes for your body.
After all, isn't life worth more than food?
And isn't the body worth more than clothes?
Look at the birds; they do not plant seeds,
gather a harvest and put it in barns; yet your
Father in heaven takes care of them! Aren't
you worth much more than birds? Can any of
you live a bit longer by worrying about it?

And why worry about clothes? Consider the
lilies, how they grow but they do not work to
make clothes for themselves. But I tell you,
not even King Solomon in all his glory was as
beautiful as one of these wild flowers. It is
God who clothes the wild grass. Won't He be
all the more sure to clothe you? What little
trust you have!

Matthew 6:25–30

If I Should Wake Before I Die

FAITH AND BELIEF

*Faith and belief and vision are the means
by which the goal of holiness is reached.
Through them the Holy Spirit leads you
to the real world, and away from all illusions
where your faith was laid. This is His direction;
the only one He ever sees. And when you
wander, He reminds you there is but one.
His faith and His belief and vision are all
for you. And when you have accepted them,
completely, instead of yours, you will have
need of them no longer. For faith and vision
and belief are meaningful only before
the state of certainty is reached. In Heaven
they are unknown. Yet Heaven is reached
through them.*

*It is impossible that the Son (child) of God
lack faith, but he can choose where he
would have it be. Faithlessness is not
a lack of faith, but faith in nothing.*

Course in Miracles: Text, Ch. 21, Page 421

Recommended Books on Death, Dying and Spiritual Awakening

Anderson, Alan, C., *The Problem Is God—The Selection and Care of Your Personal God,* Stillpoint Publishing, Walpole, NH, 1984

Attenborough, Richard, (Editor) *The Words of Gandhi,* Newmarket Press, New York City, NY, 1982

Barks, Coleman (Translator), *The Essential Rumi,* Harper Collins Publisher, New York, NY, 1995

Bertman, Sandra, *Facing Death—Images, Insights, and Interventions,* Hemisphere Publishing Corporation, New York, NY, 1991

Bly, Robert (Editor), *The Soul Is Here For Its Own Joy,* Ecco Press, Hopewell, NJ, 1995

Bly, Robert, *What Have I Ever Lost by Dying,* Harper Collins Publisher, New York, NY, 1992

Boerstler, Richard, *Letting Go—A Holistic & Meditative Approach to Living & Dying,* Associates in Thanatology, South Yarmouth, MA, 1985

Bragdon, Emma, *The Call of Spiritual Emergency—From Personal Crisis to Personal Transformation,* Harper and Row, Publishers, San Francisco, CA, 1990

Chimnoy, Sri, *Beyond Within—A Philosophy for the Inner Life,* Agni Press, Jamaica, NY, 1988

Cohen, Alan, *The Dragon Doesn't Live Here Anymore— Loving Fully, Living Freely,* Alan Cohen Publications, Somerset, NJ, 1990

Colegrave, Sukie, *By Way of Pain—A Passage into Self,* Park Street Press, Rochester, VT, 1988

Da Avabhasa, *Easy Death,* The Dawn Horse Press, Clearlake, CA, 1991, Second Edition

Dachman, Ken, and Lyons, John, *You Can Relieve Pain,* Harper and Row Publishers, New York, NY, 1990

Dass, Ram, *Journey of Awakening —A Meditators Guidebook,* Bantam Books, New York, NY, 1985

Doore, Gary, (Editor), *What Survives? Contemporary Explorations of Life After Death,* Jeremy P. Tarcher, Inc., Los Angeles, CA, 1990

Enright, D. J., *The Oxford Book of Death,* Oxford University Press, Oxford, NY, 1983

Fichter, Joseph, *Religion and Pain—The Spiritual Dimensions of Health Care,* Crossroad Publishers, New York, NY, 1981

Recommended Books on Death, Dying and Spiritual Awakening

Fleming, Ursula (Editor), *Meister Eckhart—The Man From Whom God Nothing Hid*, Templegate Publishers, Springfield, IL, 1988

Foos-Graber, Anya, *Deathing—An Intelligent Alternative for the Final Moments of Life*, Nicolas-Hays, Inc., York Beach, ME, 1989

Fox, Matthew, *Meditations with Meister Eckhart*, Bear & Company, Santa Fe, NM, 1983

Fremantle, Francesca, & Trungpa, Chogyam (Translators), *The Tibertan Book of the Dead*, Shambhala Publications, Boston, MA, 1975

Gawain, Shakti, *Creative Visualization*, Whatever Publishing, Mikll Valley, CA, 1978

Gendler, J. Ruth, *Changing Light—The Eternal Cycle of Night and Day*, Harper-Collins Publishers, New York City, NY, 1991

Guntzelman, Joan, *Blessed Grieving—Reflections of Life's Losses*, Saint Mary's Press, Christian Brothers Publications, Winona, MN, 1994

Hampton, Charles, *The Transition Called Death—A Recurring Experience*, The Theosophical Publishing House, Wheaton, IL, 1943

Hifler, Joyce, *Put Your Mind At Ease*, Abingdon Press, Nashville, TN, 1983

Holland, Samuel, *Meditation for Transformation*, Altan Press, Los Gatos, CA, 1989

Jampolsky, Gerald and Cirincione, Diane, *Wake-Up Calls*, Hay House, Inc., Carson, CA, 1992

Jampolsky, Lee, *The Art of Trust—Healing Your Heart* and Opening Your Mind, Celestial Arts Publishing, Berkeley, CA, 1994

Kapleau, Philip, *The Wheel of Life and Death*, Anchor Books-Doubleday, New York City, NY, 1989

Khan, Pir Vilayat, *The Call of the Dervish*, Omega Publications, New Lebanon, NY, 1981

Kornfield, Jack, *A Path With Heart*, Bantam Books, New York City, NY, 1993

Kubler-Ross, Elisabeth, *Death—The Final Stage of Growth*, Simon & Schuster, Inc. New York City, NY, 1975

Kubler-Ross, Elisabeth, *On Life After Death*, Celestial Arts Publications, Berkeley, CA, 1991

Kubler-Ross, Elisabeth, *To Live Until We Say Good-Bye*, Prentice-Hall, Inc., Englewood Cliffs, NJ, 1978

Recommended Books on Death, Dying and Spiritual Awakening

Kushner, Harold, *When Bad Things Happen to Good People,* Avon Books, New York City, NY, 1981

Levine, Stephen, *Guided Meditations, Explorations, and Healings,* Anchor Books, Doubleday, New York, NY, 1991

Levine, Stephen, *A Gradual Awakening,* Anchor Press-Doubleday, Garden City, NY, 1989

Levine, Stephen, *Healing Into Life and Death,* Anchor Press-Doubleday, Garden City, NY, 1987

Levine, Stephen, *Meetings at the Edge,* Anchor Press-Doubleday, Garden City, NY, 1984

Levine, Stephen, *Who Dies?,* Anchor Press-Doubleday, Garden City, NY, 1982

Linn, Mary Jane, Dennis, & Matthew, *Healing the Dying,* Paulist Press, New York City, NY, 1979

Lukeman Brenda, *Embarkations—A Guide to Dealing with Death & Parting,* Prentice-Hall Press, Englewood Cliffs, NJ, 1982

MacDonald, George, *Proving the Unseen,* Ballantine Books, New York City, NY, 1989

McClelland, Robert, W., God, *Our Loving Enemy,* Abingdon Press, Nashville, TN, 1982

Mello, Anthony de, *Sadhana—A Way to God,* Image Books, Garden City, NY, 1984

Menten, Ted, *Gentle Closings—How to Say Goodbye to Someone You Love,* Running Press, Philadelphia, PA, 1991

Mitchell, Kenneth & Anderson, Herbert, *All Our Losses—All Our Griefs,* Westminster Press, Philadelphia, PA, 1983

Mitchell, Stephen (Editor), *The Enlightened Heart—An Anthology of Sacred Poetry,* Harper & Row Publishers, New York, NY, 1989

Mitchell, Stephen (Editor), *The Enlightened Mind—An Anthology of Sacred Prose,* Harper-Collins Publishers, New York, NY, 1991

Murphet, Howard, *Beyond Death—The Undiscovered Country,* The Theosophical Publishing House, Wheaton, IL, 1990

Nisker, Wes "Scoop," *Crazy Wisdom,* Ten Speed Press, Berkeley, CA, 1990

Nouwen, Henri, *With Open Hands,* Ave Maria Press, Notre Dame, IN, 1972

Recommended Books on Death, Dying and Spiritual Awakening

Pearsall, Paul, *Making Miracles,* Prentice Hall Press, New York City, NY, 1991

Rajneesh, Bhagwan, Shree, *The Book of the Secrets,* Harper Colophon Books, Harper & Row Publishers, New York, NY, 1976

Reyes, Benito, *Conscious Dying—Psychology of Death and Guidebook to Liberation,* World University of American, Ojai, CA, 1986

Rilke, Rainer Maria, *Stories of God, Translation by M.D. Herter Norton,* W. W. Norton Company, New York, NY, 1963

Rinpoche, Sogyal, *The Tibetan Book of Living and Dying,* Harper, San Francisco, CA, 1992

Rodegast, Pat and Stanton, Judith, (Compilers), *Emmanuel's Book,* Bantam Books, New York, NY, 1987

Starr, Jonathan, (Editor), *Two Suns Rising—An Anthology of Eastern and Western Mystical Writings,* Bantam Books, New York, NY, 1992

Sujata, *Beginning to See,* Apple Pie Books, San Francisco, CA, 1987

Tart, Charles, T., *Waking Up—Overcoming the Obstacles to Human Potential,* New Science Library, Shambhala, Boston, MA, 1986

Trout, Susan, *To See Differently—Personal Growth and Being of Service Through Attitudinal Healing,* Three Roses Press, Washington, D.C., 1990

Vaughn, Frances, and Walsh, Roger, *A Gift of Healing—Selections from A Course In Miracles,* Jeremy P. Tarcher, Los Angeles, CA, 1988

Vaughn, Frances, and Walsh, Roger, *A Gift of Peace—Selections from A Course In Miracles,* Jeremy P. Tarcher, Los Angeles, CA, 1986

Watts, Alan, *OM—Creative Meditations,* Celestial Arts Publishing, Berkeley, CA, 1980

Yancey, Philip, *Where is God When It Hurts?,* Zondervan Publishing House, Grand Rapids, Michigan, 1977

Young, Alan, *Spiritual Healing—Miracle or Mirage?,* DeVorss & Company, Marina del Rey, CA, 1981

Zukav, Gary, *The Seat of the Soul,* Simon and Schuster, New York City, NY, 1989